P9-DHA-382

## Apple Pro Training Series
# Color

Michael Wohl / David Gross

Apple
Certified

Apple Pro Training Series: Color
Michael Wohl, David Gross
Copyright © 2008 by Michael Wohl and David Gross

Published by Peachpit Press. For information on Peachpit Press books, contact:

Peachpit Press
1249 Eighth Street
Berkeley, CA 94710
(510) 524-2178
Fax: (510) 524-2221
http://www.peachpit.com
To report errors, please send a note to errata@peachpit.com.
Peachpit Press is a division of Pearson Education.

**Contributing Writer, Lesson 10:** Tony Huet
**Apple Series Editor:** Serena Herr
**Project Editor:** Stephen Nathans-Kelly
**Production Coordinator:** Laurie Stewart, Happenstance Type-O-Rama
**Technical Editor:** Robbie Carman
**Technical Reviewers:** Tom Edgar, Tony Huet
**Copy Editors:** Dave Awl, Elissa Rabellino
**Compositor:** Chris Gillespie, Happenstance Type-O-Rama
**Media Producer:** Eric Geoffroy
**Indexer:** Jack Lewis
**Cover Illustration:** Kent Oberheu
**Cover Production:** Happenstance Type-O-Rama

ISBN 13: 978-0-321-50911-6
ISBN 10: 0-321-50911-0
9 8 7 6 5 4 3 2 1
Printed and bound in the United States of America

**Acknowledgments** Special thanks to Lachlan Milne, *www.lachlanmilne. com,* for his help with the planning and execution of the book, his generous sharing of his experience with both traditional color grading and digital intermediates, and, of course, his award-winning cinematography.

Thanks to our generous footage providers, Hugh Miller, *www.hughmiller.com.au*; Nathan Tomlinson, *www.xtremefreelance.com.au;* Anthony Rose, Caroline David, and Paul Friedmann of Flying Fish, Sydney, *www.flyingfish.co.nz;* Ben Blick-Hodge and Jo Sudol of Definition Films, *www.definitionfilms.com;* Mark Furmie and Carl Robertson, *www.filmgraphics.com*; Anne Robinson of Cutting Edge Post in Sydney, *www.cuttingedge.com.au*; and Ben Briand and Pip Smart of Cherub Pictures, *www.cherubpictures.com.au.*

Thanks for technical assistance and equipment to Warren Lynch of Intercolour Australia; Stuart Harris, Peter Belton, and Michael Frew of Apple Australia; Peter Sintras of Sony BMG Music Australia; Greg Clarke of Channel Seven Sport; Paul Saccone, Steve Bayes, Kirk Paulsen, and Patty Montesion of Apple; Olivier Jean, Peter Mousis, and Arthur Pennas of Powermedia Systems, Sydney; and Roger Savage, Bruce Emery, and Jennifer Lum of Soundfirm Sydney, Fox Studios Australia, *www.soundfirm.com.au.*

Personal thanks to Deanna Lomonaco, Patrick Rodden, Jenni Lees, Bernard Gross, Carolyn Gross, and Woodrow Gross.

# Contents at a Glance

# Table of Contents

# Getting Started

Welcome to the official Apple Pro Training Series course for Color. This comprehensive overview of Apple's new color grading software will broaden your skills as a post-production expert, adding color correction and grading to your arsenal of tools. While you work through the exercises in the lessons, you'll learn not only the many correction and grading features of Color, but also how to perform those tasks in real-world situations.

Whether you're an expert at using Final Cut Pro's built-in color correction tools or a newcomer to the whole Final Cut Studio, this book will help you master Color while improving your color-correction techniques.

# The Methodology

This is, first and foremost, a hands-on course. Every exercise is designed to get you creating professional-quality color grades in Color as quickly as possible. Each lesson builds on previous lessons to guide you through the program's functions and capabilities. However, if you're already familiar with this powerful new tool, you can also go directly to a specific section and focus on that topic because each lesson is self-contained.

## Course Structure

The book is designed to improve your skills both as a colorist and as an operator of this versatile software. The software interface is divided into eight "rooms." The most common workflow moves clips through the rooms in more or less sequential order. This is also the model for how the book is organized.

The first lesson gives an overview of the entire Color workflow, including a brief introduction to each of the rooms and the types of tasks typically performed there. This lesson also details the "round-trip" workflow from Final Cut Pro to Color and back to Final Cut Pro. Most editors who use Final Cut Studio will employ this workflow, where projects are edited in Final Cut Pro, sent to Color for grading and finishing, and then returned to Final Cut Pro for final output.

The rest of the book walks you through each of the main rooms and goes into significant detail on both how to use each of the many controls as well as which tools and techniques to apply given the specific shots and circumstances of your projects.

The lessons are grouped into the following categories:

### Quick Start Overview, Lesson 1

Many people new to Color aren't sure exactly what it's for and what it's capable of. This overview lesson is a brief survey of the entire workflow, highlighting some common tricks and techniques along the way. This section also covers the round-trip workflow from and to Final Cut Pro.

### Primary Color Grading, Lesson 2

The primary grading lesson covers the most common color-correcting tools and techniques you'll use to improve the look of virtually every clip in your project.

**Secondary Color Grading, Lessons 3–4**

The secondary grading lessons are where you really customize the look and style of each shot. You'll learn how to affect different parts of the image discretely and apply multiple grades simultaneously.

**Grade Management, Lesson 5**

While learning to grade individual shots is essential, in the real world you'll be faced with whole projects containing many shots that require the matching and repetition of grades. Color has many tools to handle scene-to-scene color matching and reapplying or batch-applying grades, and this lesson shows you how to use them.

**Color Effects and Recipes, Lessons 6–7**

Moving beyond the basic types of color correction and grading, these lessons introduce you to Color's powerful and flexible effects tools, and teach you how to build your own unique effects using the built-in presets as your starting point. Lesson 7 contains a set of recipes for creating popular and useful effects and "looks" that are sure to wow your clients.

**Advanced Techniques, Lessons 8–9**

Once you master the basic tools Color has to offer, you'll likely begin craving the additional control made possible by employing keyframes, pan and scan motion effects, and motion tracking. These topics are all covered thoroughly in this section.

**Finishing and Rendering, Lesson 10**

Color is a precision tool intended for professional environments with stringent delivery requirements. This section covers Broadcast Safe settings, rendering options, and final output decisions.

## Using the DVD Book Files

The *Apple Pro Training Series: Color* DVD (included with the book) contains the project files you'll use for each lesson, as well as media files that contain the video content you'll need for each exercise. After you transfer the files to your hard drive, each lesson will instruct you in the use of the project and media files.

### Installing the Color Lesson Files

On the DVD, you'll find a folder titled Color_Book_Files, which contains individual subfolders for each lesson in the book. Each subfolder contains a lesson file (either a Final Cut Pro or Color project file) and a Media folder containing all the clips required for that lesson.

**1** Insert the *Apple Pro Training Series: Color* DVD into your DVD drive.

**2** Drag the Color Book Files folder from the DVD to your hard drive to copy it. The Media folders contain about 3 GB of media in total.

Each lesson will explain which files to open for that lesson's exercises.

### Reconnecting Media

When copying files from the DVD to your hard drive, Color will lose the link between the project files and the associated media. This will result in the clips appearing "offline" in the Color project. Each lesson contains specific steps to remedy this, but here are the basic steps you'll apply each time you open a new Color project.

**1** After opening each Color project, the Timeline will show all the clips in red with a red X across the clip icon. Choose File > Reconnect Media.

A Choose Media Path dialog opens.

**2** Navigate (using the Parent Directory button in the upper left) to the media folder for the current lesson and click Choose.

You don't need to select an individual file; just choosing the directory that contains the media is sufficient.

When the link between the project file and the media file is reestablished, Color will be able to access the media within the project.

## System Requirements

Before using *Apple Pro Training Series: Color,* you should have a working knowledge of your Macintosh and the Mac OS X operating system. Make sure that you know how to use the mouse and standard menus and commands; and also how to open, save, and close files. If you need to review these techniques, see the printed or online documentation included with your system. For the basic system requirements for Color, refer to the Final Cut Studio 2 documentation.

### Three-Button Mouse Required

Color makes extensive use of a multi-button mouse, and many functions and tasks are impossible or at least very inconvenient without a right mouse button and a middle-mouse button/scroll wheel. While you can almost always use Control-click as a replacement for a right-click, there is no keyboard equivalent for the middle-click or the scroll wheel.

The Apple Mighty Mouse is an excellent multi-button mouse to use with Color, although many third-party mice will work as well. Regardless of the mouse you use, be sure that your Keyboard and Mouse settings in your System Preferences are configured so the right button is set to "Secondary Button" and the middle button is set to "Button 3."

## About the Apple Pro Training Series

*Apple Pro Training Series: Color* is part of the official training series for Apple Pro applications developed by experts in the field. The series is used in Apple-certified training worldwide, and is also the market-leading series for self-paced readers who want to learn Apple Pro applications on their own. Because Color is a new application introduced in Final Cut Studio 2, this book covers the fundamental concepts and features you'll need to master the program as a first-time user. However, it's also suitable for readers familiar with Final Cut Studio 1 or with Silicon Color Final Touch.

Although each lesson provides step-by-step instructions for creating specific projects, there's room for exploration and experimentation. However, try to follow the book from start to finish, or at least complete the first three sections before jumping around. Each lesson concludes with a review section summarizing what you've covered.

## Apple Pro Certification Program

The Apple Pro Training and Certification Programs are designed to keep you at the forefront of Apple's digital media technology while giving you a competitive edge in today's ever-changing job market. Whether you're an editor, graphic designer, sound designer, special effects artist, or teacher, these training tools are meant to help you expand your skills.

Upon completing the course material in this book, you can become Apple Pro Certified by taking the certification exam at an Apple Authorized Training Center. Certification is offered in Final Cut Pro, Motion, Color, Soundtrack Pro, DVD Studio Pro, Shake, and Logic Pro. Apple Certification gives you official recognition of your knowledge of Apple's professional applications while allowing you to market yourself to employers and clients as a skilled, pro-level user of Apple products.

To find an Authorized Training Center near you, go to www.apple.com/software/pro/training.

For those who prefer to learn in an instructor-led setting, Apple offers training courses at Apple Authorized Training Centers worldwide. These courses, which use the Apple Pro Training Series books as their curriculum, are taught by Apple Certified Trainers and balance concepts and lectures with hands-on labs and exercises. Apple Authorized Training Centers for Pro products have been carefully selected and have met Apple's highest standards in all areas, including facilities, instructors, course delivery, and infrastructure. The goal of the program is to offer Apple customers, from beginners to the most seasoned professionals, the highest-quality training experience.

## Resources

*Apple Pro Training Series: Color* is not intended as a comprehensive reference manual, nor does it replace the documentation that comes with the application. For comprehensive information about program features, refer to these resources:

▶ The Reference Guide. Accessed through the Color Help menu, the Reference Guide contains a complete description of all features.

▶ Apple's website: www.apple.com

# 1

**Lesson Files**   Color Book Files > Lesson Files > Lesson 01 > Overview.fcp

**Time**   This lesson takes approximately 90 minutes to complete.

**Goals**   Send a sequence from Final Cut Pro to Color

Navigate projects in the Color Timeline

Tour the rooms of the Color interface

Explore Color's task-based workflow

Set preferences for your sequence

Experiment with simple color adjustments

# Working with the Color Interface

For many editors, color correction is the missing piece of the digital puzzle. Until recently, editors had to rely on professional colorists to grade their projects. With the addition of Color, Final Cut Studio 2 becomes the first production suite that brings professional color correction to the masses. The aim of this book is to penetrate the mystery of color grading while you learn how to use Color.

In this lesson, you'll send a sequence from Final Cut Pro to Color, tour the Color interface, familiarize yourself with Color's intuitive task-based workflow, set preferences for your sequence, and experiment with some simple adjustments while you get to know the most important tabs, or *rooms*, in the Color interface.

## Setting Up Your Computer

First of all, ensure that your system meets the minimum hardware requirements for using Color effectively. To display images properly, Color requires at least the standard graphics card that is included in any Mac Pro, 24-inch iMac, 2.5 GHz or faster Power Mac G5 Quad, or 17-inch MacBook Pro. Also, to show the entire Color interface, your display must be set to a minimum resolution of 1680 x 1050 pixels. A lower resolution compromises the interface by cropping some of its panels and shrinking interface text to an illegible size.

Additionally, to access Color's full functionality, you'll need a three-button mouse. This includes the Mighty Mouse that is provided with the desktop computers listed above, or any three-button, Macintosh-compatible mouse. To configure a three-button mouse, go to your computer's System Preferences, and in the Keyboard & Mouse pane set the left button to Primary Button, the right button to Secondary Button, and the middle button to Button 3.

## Setting Up a Project

Before you start color correcting, you'll send a sequence of three clips from Final Cut Pro to Color. This is a common, real-world workflow that you're likely to use for all of your sequences.

1   In the Finder, navigate to Color Book Files > Lesson Files > Lesson 01.

2   Double-click **Overview.fcp** to open the project, in Final Cut Pro.

The Lesson01 sequence should be open in the Canvas and Timeline.

3   Examine the three clips in the sequence. Each one displays common problems that can be corrected using Color.

The first shot, **CarShotWide**, is overexposed, and too bright. As a result, the image lacks a wide *tonal range*, which is the range of brightness from the lightest white to the darkest black.

Images with a narrow tonal range tend to lack depth and look flat. Also, they'll lack brighter area details—such as the texture of the headlights in the current image—and the shadows won't be dark enough to look natural. Soon you'll learn how a simple adjustment in Color can dramatically improve this shot.

The second shot, **CarTrackMS**, is underexposed, and too dark. Like the previous shot, it lacks a wide tonal range and looks flat. The texture in the car's tire treads is lost, and the white areas appear more gray than white. You'll also learn how Color can easily correct this image.

The third shot, **CarGrillCU**, has an improper color balance, and is too yellow.

The fourth shot, **GreenDoorPeek**, also has reduced contrast and provides an opportunity to work with human flesh tones, which have special importance for colorists.

One of the most common goals of color correction is to restore the original look of a scene so that the colors of objects are represented accurately. For a commercial car shot like this one, accurate color representation is critical because your clients will want their products to be shown properly and pleasingly. You'll use Color's image-analysis tools to help you recognize and neutralize such problems.

To perform all of these corrections, move the entire sequence into Color.

**4**    Choose File > Send to > Color.

> **NOTE** ▶ If the Send to > Color command is dimmed, verify that either the Canvas or Timeline window is active.

The Send To Color dialog appears.

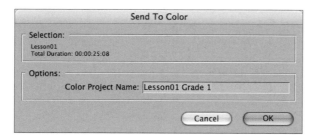

**5**    In the Color Project Name field, type *Lesson01 Grade 1*, and click OK.

Color will open automatically, and an identical sequence will appear in the Color Timeline.

The Color project is created and saved in your Documents > Color Documents folder with a *.colorproj* extension.

> **NOTE** ▶ That default location can be changed in the User Prefs tab of the Setup room.

**TIP** ▶ Alternatively, you could launch Color, create a new project, and import your clips, but sending to Color directly from Final Cut Pro maintains your editing decisions, and processes only the edited portions of the clips in your sequence. Additionally, many settings from Final Cut Pro's motion tab and Color Correction 3-way filter will be translated directly to Color.

Final Cut Pro and Color communicate with each other through a language called *XML*. When you send your sequence from Final Cut Pro to Color, the software uses XML to track information about all of the video, audio, and effects editing you did in your Final Cut Pro sequence. Color reads this XML to re-create your sequence in the Color Timeline. If you have any audio clips, effects (except the Color Corrector 3-way filter), Motion or LiveType projects or templates, generators, or stills in your Final Cut Pro sequence, Color will temporarily ignore them or they will appear as gaps in the Color Timeline. But because all of those elements are still described in XML, they will reappear when you return your rendered clips to Final Cut Pro.

The round-trip workflow between Final Cut Pro and Color saves you the time and trouble of having to import individual clips into Color before you can begin your color grading. Also, since the edited version of your footage is sent to Color, media management becomes easier because Color is working only with your used media.

## Understanding the Eight Rooms: Color's Task-Based Workflow

The Color interface is divided into two windows: the Viewer and the Composer. In the Viewer window, you'll see your video images, as well as the video scopes. In the Composer window, you'll find the Timeline, as well as all the color-correction controls, which are divided into eight tabs called *rooms*. Each room performs a different function in the color workflow, and they're arranged from left to right in the order in which you'll typically apply corrections. Additional tabs appear at the bottom of some rooms and access additional tools and controls. These tabs are also arranged in the order in which you would typically use them.

Viewer window          Composer window          Tabs for each of the eight rooms

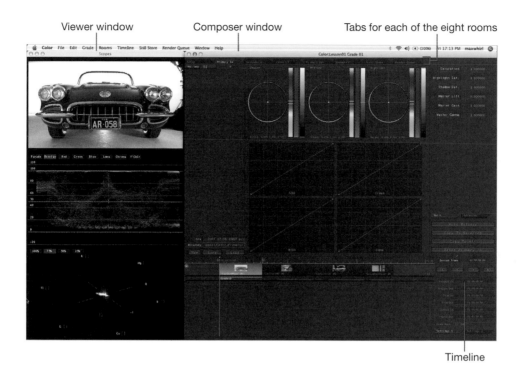

Timeline

### Setup Room

In the Setup room, you customize user preferences and project settings, such as interface colors, Auto Save, and Broadcast Safe specifications. The Setup room also contains areas in which you can view a sequential list or graphical display of all your shots, group shots together that will require the same corrections, and save entire grades for future use.

### Primary In Room

In the Primary In room, you begin your color corrections, making adjustments that affect the entire image, such as contrast and color balancing.

### Secondaries Room

In the Secondaries room, you apply color corrections to specific portions of the image, rather than to the entire image. For example, if you'd like to enhance only the color of a sky or a person's face, you would perform that work in the Secondaries Room.

### Color FX Room

In the Color FX room, you combine and apply imaging filters to create styled looks using a node-based system. Effects that you build in the Color FX room can be saved and applied to future shots.

### Primary Out Room

The Primary Out room is almost identical to the Primary In room except that the final corrections made here are applied after the changes that were made in all the other rooms. Final tweaks can best be made in the Primary Out room.

### Geometry Room

In the Geometry room, you adjust the size and position of the frame, draw custom shapes for isolating secondary color corrections, and motion track shapes to moving objects.

### Still Store

In the Still Store, you can save freeze frames of shots and use a split-screen display to compare them with other shots in the Timeline.

### Render Queue

In the Render Queue, you choose which shots you want to render before returning the sequence to Final Cut Pro.

## Navigating Your Sequence

Before you can utilize the powerful grading tools in Color, you have to understand which clips will be affected as you adjust Color's controls. Color's Timeline is visible no matter which room is active, and it provides an overview of your entire project. When you use the Send To Color command from Final Cut Pro, your entire Final Cut Pro Timeline is replicated in Color, including multiple layers and transitions with handles (although Color does not display or render transition effects).

### Navigating Clip to Clip

The Color Timeline navigation is similar, but not identical, to the Timeline navigation in Final Cut Pro. Navigation buttons are located to the right of Color's main Timeline display.

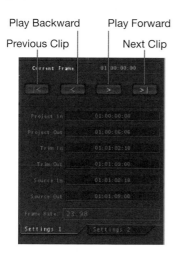

1   Press Home to move the playhead to the beginning of the sequence.

2   Click the Next Clip button (or press the Down Arrow key) to jump from clip to clip.

3   Click the Previous Clip button (or press the Up Arrow key) to move backward one clip at a time.

4   Press the Left and Right arrows to step through individual frames of the current clip.

**TIP** ▶ You can also drag the playhead in the ruler area to move to a new frame or to scrub through your clips.

It's very important to understand that the Timeline playhead position determines which clip is affected by changes you make in any of the color-correction rooms. Moving from clip to clip will update the controls in the rooms to show the settings that are currently active for that clip. Active clips are displayed in a lighter color than the other clips.

While you can select a clip in the Timeline, doing so will not activate it for grading. However, double-clicking a clip will cause the playhead to jump to that clip, thereby selecting it and also activating it for grading.

5  Double-click the second clip, **CarTrackMS**, to select it and activate it for grading.

**Playing Clips**

It is absolutely critical to preview your clips often during color grading work. Remember, you're working on moving images; while you make adjustments that might appear perfect on a single frame, other sections of the same clip may require different adjustments.

Color has two playback modes. In the default mode, playback loops around the current clip; in the alternate mode, playback moves from clip to clip across an entire sequence or a marked area (as it does in Final Cut Pro). You can verify which mode you're in by checking the positions of the In and Out points in the Timeline ruler.

The In and Out points indicate which area of the Timeline will be looped when you begin playback.

While Play Forward and Play Backward buttons are present in the Timeline navigation area, it's far more intuitive to use the familiar keyboard shortcuts: spacebar, J, K, and L.

**NOTE ▶** The J, K, and L shortcut keys work only when the Timeline is active.

1   Press the spacebar to start playback.

The clip plays and loops until you press the spacebar a second time.

2   Choose Timeline > Toggle Playback Mode (or press Shift-Command-M).

The In and Out points move to encompass the entire sequence.

3   Press the spacebar again.

Now the sequence plays across multiple clips.

### Locking and Hiding Tracks

Color's Timeline includes a wide variety of editing tools, including ripple, roll, slip, add edit, and others that you probably use in Final Cut Pro. However, editing in Color will undermine your ability to round-trip between Color and Final Cut Pro.

Because of this, when a Color project is created using the Send to > Color command in Final Cut Pro (as previously described), Color automatically locks the Timeline tracks to prevent any accidental changes.

You can tell if a track is locked by the presence of a lock icon in the upper left corner of the track. You won't be able to make any editorial changes to the clips on that track unless you unlock it.

Lock icon

Tracks can be locked or unlocked by right-clicking (or Control-clicking) the track and, from the shortcut menu, choosing Lock Track or Unlock Track.

Attempting to unlock a track triggers a warning about Final Cut Pro interoperability.

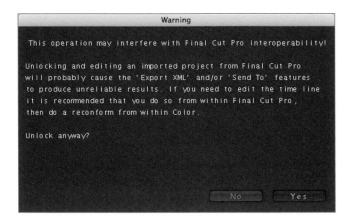

Also present in that shortcut menu is the Hide Track command. Hiding a track disables clips on that track from appearing in the Viewer or in the grading rooms. This command is similar to clicking the Enable button in the Final Cut Pro Timeline track header area.

1   Right-click the track in the Timeline.

2   From the shortcut menu, choose Hide Track.

The track is hidden and the Viewer displays black. Color correction cannot be applied to clips on a hidden track.

3   Right-click the track again, and from the shortcut menu, choose Show Track.

**NOTE** ▶ Hidden tracks can still be rendered, and when the sequence is returned to Final Cut Pro, tracks hidden in Color will not automatically be hidden in Final Cut Pro.

### Zooming In and Out

Although editing clips in the Color Timeline is a rare occurrence, it is common to zoom in and out to better see the boundaries of the clips you're grading.

1   Choose Timeline > Zoom In or press Command-+ (plus).

The Timeline zooms in.

2   Choose Timeline > Zoom Out or press Command–– (minus).

The Timeline zooms back out.

This is a familiar and easy way to zoom in and out on the Timeline. Color provides another way to zoom, but it's hidden in a nontraditional place. If you right-click the Timeline ruler and drag, Color enables a zooming shortcut function.

3   Right-click the ruler area of the Timeline and don't release the mouse button.

4   With the right mouse button still held down, drag right to zoom in and drag left to zoom out.

### Resizing Tracks

In addition to zooming in and out on the temporal scale, you may also want to enlarge your Timeline tracks to see the thumbnails more clearly, or reduce the tracks to view more of them simultaneously.

Color tracks can be resized in a similar manner to the way they are in Final Cut Pro.

1   Click the black line beneath the clip icons in the Timeline.

**NOTE ▶** Don't click the bar beneath the grade tabs as this expands the area showing the grades and corrections applied to the clips.

2   Drag the line up or down to enlarge or shrink all Timeline tracks.

**TIP ▶** If you have multiple tracks, all tracks are resized together. Unlike Final Cut Pro, Color provides no way to enlarge or shrink individual tracks.

### Managing Grades in the Timeline

Below the tracks containing the video clips, the Timeline includes an additional area to display what grade is currently applied to the active clip. This is called the Grades track.

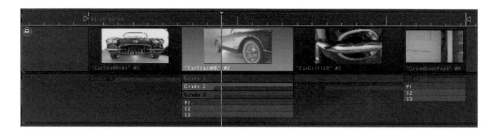

For more information on organizing and managing grades, see Lesson 5.

**NOTE** ▶ The image above includes grades and correction settings that will not appear in your project file.

## Exploring the Setup Room

In the Setup room, you'll set all of your project preferences. It's critical to choose project preferences early in the process to ensure that you'll see and render your shots properly.

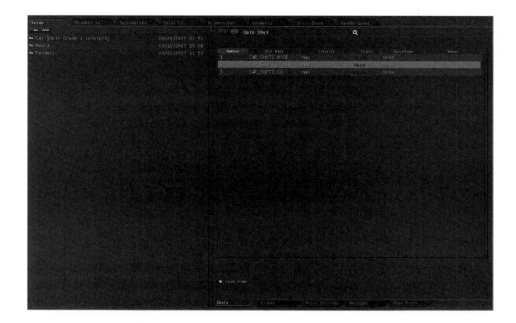

### The Shots Tab

1   At the top of the Composer window, click the Setup tab.

The Setup room has its own set of tabs at the bottom, with which you can make additional modifications. The tabs are arranged left to right in the order in which you typically will use them.

2   At the bottom of the Setup room, click the Shots tab.

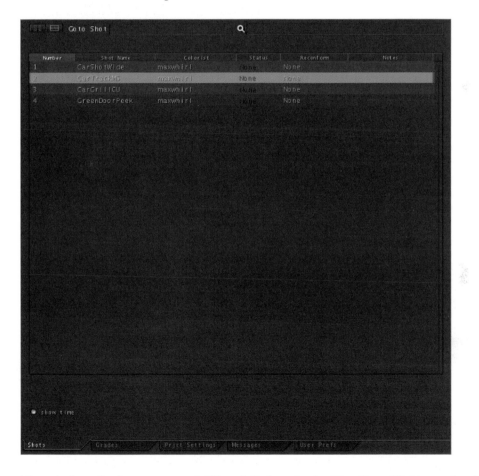

The window displays a sequential list of all shots in the Timeline. Clicking a shot in the list selects the clip in the Timeline.

## The Grades Tab

**1**    At the bottom of the Setup room, click the Grades tab.

Here is where you save favorite *grades* and quickly apply them to other shots in the Timeline. A grade contains settings from all of the other Color rooms. Room-specific settings also can be saved (within each room) and are called *corrections* rather than *grades*.

## The Project Settings Tab

**1**    Click the Project Settings tab. (On smaller screens, this tab's name may be abbreviated as Prjct Settings.)

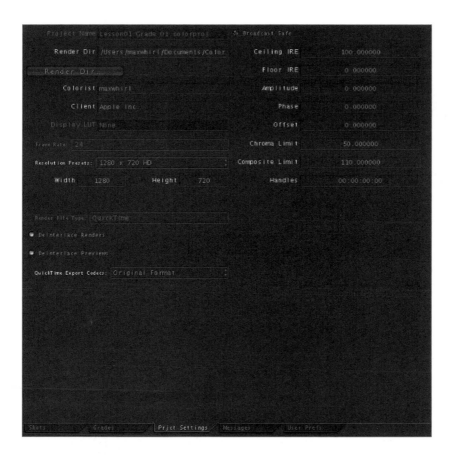

Here, you customize settings specific to the current project. Many of the settings deal with the technical specifications of video clips, but other fields are available to enter the names of the colorist and the client.

2   In the Colorist field, type your name; then press the Tab key to move to the Client field. Type *IndyCorp* and press the Enter key.

The Broadcast Safe checkbox (in the top right of the Project Settings tab) is selected by default. This checkbox instructs Color to automatically ensure that your corrections don't exceed the signal specification standards of broadcast television.

Although this is helpful, it simply clips values that exceed the legal limit, which is not the most desirable way to limit the signal. For more specific control over your broadcast-safe settings, you typically use the Primary Out room, described later in this lesson.

## The Messages Tab

**1** Click the Messages tab.

The Messages tab displays warnings and errors to help you troubleshoot technical problems you may encounter while working with Color. Yellow messages are warnings and red messages are errors.

**NOTE ▶** You should not see any warnings in your Messages tab. Occasional messages may appear to display the real-time playback frame rate your system is giving you, displayed in fps (frames per second), or to indicate playback mode changes and so on.

## The User Preferences Tab

**1** Click the User Prefs tab.

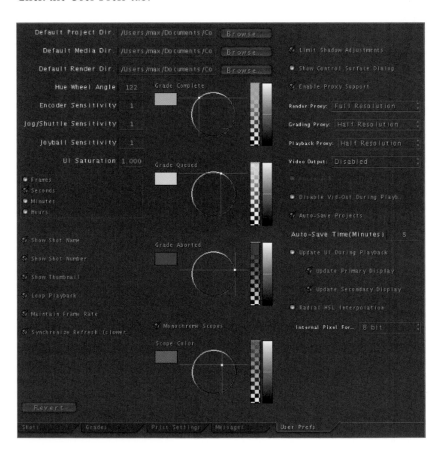

Here you customize application settings, such as interface preferences, and choose your media and project directories. The default Scope Color is orange. The grayscale gradient strip on the right controls the Scope Color's brightness. You may find that increasing the brightness improves the scopes' readability.

**2**  Drag the Contrast slider up toward white.

The scopes in the Viewer window change from orange to white.

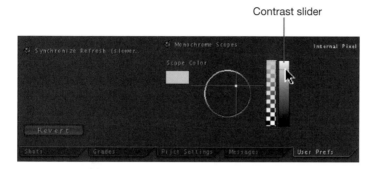

## Applying Basic Grades

The Primary In room is where color correction begins. Here, you make adjustments that change the appearance of the entire image, such as fixing poor contrast and neutralizing unwanted color casts.

**1**  Click the Timeline ruler directly above the first clip.

Changes made in any room affect the clip currently under the playhead in the Timeline.

**2**  At the top of the Composer window, click the Primary In tab.

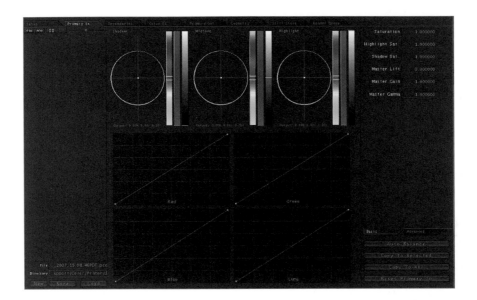

At the top half of the room are three color balance controls that control the hue and saturation of the shadows, midtones, and highlights of your current clip. These are called color balance controls. The three gradient strips to the right are sliders: The first two sliders are alternative controls for hue and saturation, and the third slider, called the contrast slider, adjusts contrast.

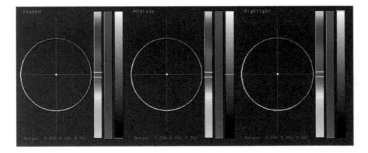

3    To familiarize yourself with this interface, move your pointer over the Highlight color balance control, and drag the crosshair inside the color balance control around the edges of the control.

Notice how the brighter areas of the image change color in the Viewer window.

4    Move your pointer over the rainbow gradient to the right of the Highlight color balance control.

This is the Highlight Hue slider. Notice the two white horizontal lines in this slider. These indicate the current highlight color.

5   Drag the Saturation slider up and down.

Notice how the image's color becomes more or less intense. As you drag, also notice how the color balance control's crosshair moves farther from and closer to the center of the balance control. This slider controls the saturation level of the color that the balance control is adding to the image.

The rightmost slider, which looks like a grayscale gradient strip, is the Highlight contrast slider, which controls the white level of the image.

6   Drag the Hue slider up and down.

Notice how the color of the image changes. As you drag, also notice how the color balance control's crosshair moves in a circular way. The Hue slider is an alternative way to adjust one aspect of the color balance control crosshair's position.

The middle gradient is the Saturation slider. This controls the intensity of the Highlight color.

7   Drag the contrast slider up and down, and notice how the image becomes brighter or darker.

There is one more important part of a color balance control control: the cyan dot in the lower-left corner.

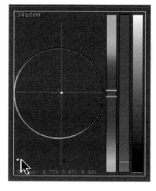

This is the color balance control's reset button.

8   Click the reset button to reset the color balance control to its default settings.

## Viewing Your Images

Before you continue, it's important to learn a little more about the Viewer window. The Viewer window displays your current clip, as well as Color's video scopes. The video scopes measure various components of your video signal. A video signal consists of two parts: *luma* and *chroma*. You can monitor those parts discretely or in useful limited combinations using different scopes.

You can configure your window layout to view multiple scopes simultaneously. There are four scopes to choose from: the Waveform Monitor, the Vectorscope, the Histogram, and the 3D Color Space Scope. Each of these scopes provides vital information that might not be entirely apparent by looking at only the video image. Additionally, each scope contains options to limit or expand what information is displayed (such as displaying red, green, and blue channels separately, or viewing the scopes in different color spaces).

In single-display mode, the Viewer window shows the video on top and has two scope areas below.

In dual-display mode, the Viewer occupies an entire screen and is divided into quadrants.

1  In the Viewer window, double-click the video image.

   The video expands to fill the entire window.

2  Double-click again to return the video image to the small size.

   You can also right-click the video to switch between full screen and quarter screen.

## Using the Waveform Monitor

The Waveform Monitor measures only the luma, or the brightness and contrast, of a video image. To comply with broadcast standards, the scope's reading, or *trace*, should generally lie between 0% and 100% on the Waveform Monitor.

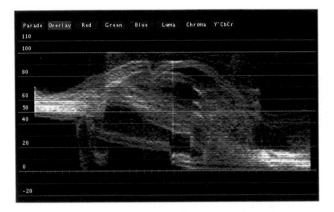

1   In the Primary In room, drag the Highlight contrast slider (the grayscale strip beside the Highlight color balance control) up and down.

Observe how the *top* of the Waveform Monitor's trace moves up and down as the *white level* of the image becomes brighter or darker.

2   Repeat this procedure with the Shadow contrast slider.

Notice how the *bottom* of the trace moves up and down as the *black level* of the image becomes brighter or darker.

3   Repeat this procedure with the Midtone contrast slider.

As you might expect, the traces in the middle of the image move toward the top or the bottom of the scope as the image grows brighter or darker. While the contrast sliders for Highlight and Shadow adjust the white and black levels, respectively, the contrast slider for Midtone controls the overall brightness and darkness of the entire image.

When you make a Midtone adjustment, it also affects the white and black levels. You will soon learn how to use all three of these sliders to correct problems with exposure. For now, let's look at how the other color balance controls affect the image.

4   Click the reset buttons for the Shadow, Midtone, and Highlight color balance controls to reset them to their default values.

**Using the Vectorscope**

The Vectorscope measures the chrominance, or hue and saturation, of a video image. The Vectorscope's overlay includes labels for the primary and secondary colors of light: red, magenta, blue, cyan, green, and yellow. When the traces in the Vectorscope extend toward one of these labels, it indicates the presence of that color in the image. The intensity of that color is represented by the distance that the trace extends from the scope's center.

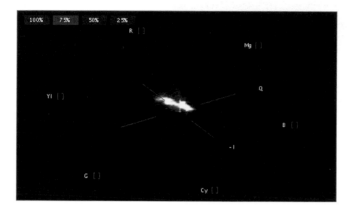

1   Drag the crosshair inside the Midtone color balance control to various positions.

As you drag, watch how the Vectorscope's trace moves toward the different color labels, indicating you are adding that color to the image.

2   Click the reset button for the Midtone color balance control to cancel this adjustment.

3   Inside the Shadow color balance control, drag the crosshair along the edges of the control.

Notice that this kind of adjustment adds the color only to the darker areas of the image. The brighter areas are only nominally affected.

4   Click the reset button for the Shadow color balance control to remove this adjustment.

5   Repeat these actions with the Highlight color balance control.

Now you're adding colors only to the image's brighter areas. The darker areas are hardly affected.

6   Click the reset button for the Highlight color balance control to cancel this adjustment.

Color includes two other scopes to aid you in your work, the Histogram and the 3D Color Space Scope. These scopes will be described in later lessons.

## Performing Secondary Grades

In the Secondaries room, you perform color adjustments on selected portions of an image rather than to an entire image.

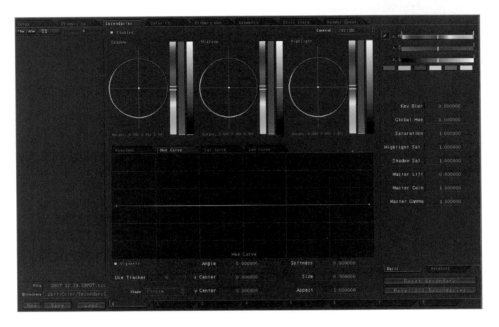

In this example, you'll isolate a specific color and perform an adjustment to that color without affecting the rest of the image.

1    In the Timeline, double-click the last clip in the sequence (**GreenDoorPeek**).

If you single click instead of double-clicking the clip will be selected, but corrections will still be applied to the clip under the playhead. Make sure the playhead is parked over the last clip and that the green door shot is visible in the Viewer window.

2    At the top of the Composer window, click the Secondaries tab.

**3**    Click the eyedropper in the upper-right corner of the Secondaries room.

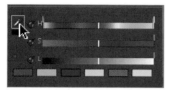

Using the eyedropper automatically enables the secondary, as indicated by the check-box in the upper-left corner of the window.

**NOTE ▶** While using the eyedropper activates the Enabled checkbox automatically, many other controls in the Secondaries room do not. If you're making secondary adjustments and don't see any effect in the Viewer, always verify that the Enabled checkbox is activated.

When you click the eyedropper, a crosshair appears in the Viewer to aid you in select-ing your desired color.

**4**    In the Viewer, drag the crosshairs across the door to select its color. Be sure to drag across the light and dark areas of the door.

As you drag, the area outside of your selection becomes desaturated. This is an indicator to help you confirm your selection. The final image will not include this desaturation.

Additionally, the center of the Secondaries room contains a preview tab that displays another copy of the clip, as well as a black-and-white image also designed to aid in identifying your selection. Areas that are white indicate the selection.

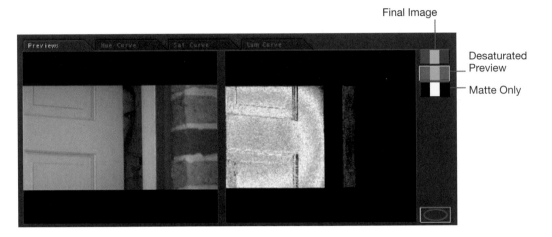

Final Image

Desaturated Preview

Matte Only

On the right side of the Previews area, three Matte Preview Mode buttons determine what is displayed in the Viewer window.

By default, the center button, Desaturated Preview, is enabled, which shows your selection in color and the rest of the image in black and white.

5   Click the bottom button, Matte Only, to display your selected pixels as white in the Viewer.

6   Click the top button, Final Image, to see the final result of your correction.

Because you haven't made any changes yet, the image in the viewer looks just like the original.

**7**   In the Midtones color balance control, drag the crosshair toward the blue edge.

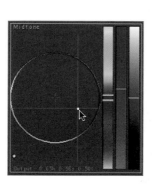 

In the Viewer, the door pixels turn blue.

**8**   Move the crosshair toward magenta, and the door turns pink.

**9**   In the lower-right corner of the Secondaries room, click the Reset All Secondaries button to reset all parameters to their default values.

The Secondaries room offers a multitude of additional controls, both for controlling the selection, and for modifying that selection to create different effects.

## Employing Color FX

In the Color FX room, you stylize shots using filters and effect presets. This room contains three panels. On the left is the Node List, which contains a wide variety of filters and preset effects. The open area in the middle of the Color FX room is the Node View, where you can string together filters to create complex and unique effects. The right section contains two tabs: Parameters, where you adjust selected filters, and Color FX Bin, which stores preset collections of nodes.

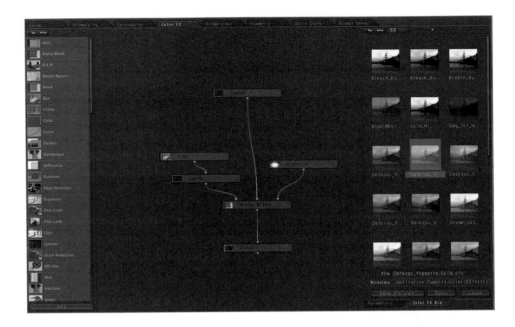

**NOTE ▶** By default, your project will not have any nodes or presets showing.

1　In the Timeline, double-click the second clip (**CarTrackMS**).

2　At the top of the Composer window, click the Color FX tab.

3　In the Node List, double-click the Duotone node.

By default, the Duotone node tints your image sepia. In the Parameters tab, there are Light Color and Dark Color controls, employing the familiar color balance control interface.

**4**  Experiment by adjusting these controls, and observe how your image is affected in the Viewer.

**5**  At the top of the Parameters tab, click the Bypass button to disable the node's effect.

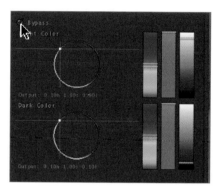

**6**  Click the Color FX Bin tab.

In this bin, you can find a variety of effects presets to perform common effects, such as bleach bypass, day for night, and myriad dream looks.

**7**  Double-click Blue_Movie_Look.

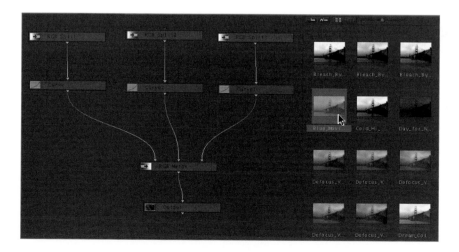

The preset automatically applies a tree of nodes to create the overall effect.

**NOTE ▶** Applying a new preset replaces the existing nodes in the Node View.

8  Double-click Bleach_Bypass_Adjustable, and notice that a different tree of nodes is applied.

9  In the Node View, drag to select all the nodes in the tree, and press Delete to remove them.

## Applying Final Touches

The fifth tab activates the Primary Out room. The controls there are nearly identical to those of the Primary In room; however, the effects are applied after the effects in the other rooms are applied. For example, if you wanted to apply several secondary corrections to parts of your image and then make a single global change to all of them, you would make that global change in the Primary Out room.

One of the most common uses for the Primary Out room is to make adjustments that address possible violations of broadcast signal requirements. While the Broadcast Safe setting in the Project Settings tab of the Setup room clips any signals that exceed the legal limit, for the best results you will want to rein in such excesses gradually to eliminate possible artifacts or strange color shifts generated by the automatic clipping.

Because changes you make in the Primary In, Secondaries, and Color FX rooms can combine and affect each other, limiting and correcting for broadcast requirements is best done after those other adjustments have been completed. The Primary Out room is the last image processing stop prior to rendering, making it the ideal room for such work.

## Panning and Scanning

In the Geometry room, an image can be resized and repositioned for a pan-and-scan effect. Also, custom shapes can be drawn here to isolate areas in the image prior to performing secondary corrections in the Secondaries room.

1   At the top of the Composer window, click the Geometry tab.

The bounding box around the image in the large preview area indicates the visible area of the frame. Inside that box, there are two additional boxes to indicate action-safe and title-safe boundaries. By changing the bounding box size and position, you can scale the image, and create "pan and scan" effects.

2   Drag any of the corners of the bounding box to adjust the size of the frame.

3   Drag the edges of the bounding box to adjust rotation.

4   Drag inside the bounding box to adjust the position of the frame.

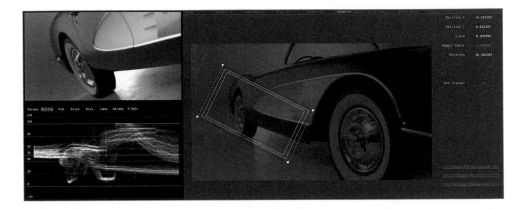

The Viewer shows the image following your adjustments. The Pan&Scan tab on the right displays the settings numerically, allowing you to enter specific values.

5   Click the Reset Geometry button at the bottom of the Pan&Scan tab to remove any changes you have made.

The Geometry room is also where you create custom shapes for limiting corrections in the Secondaries room, and where you control trackers so Color can move masks and corrections along with an object as it moves within the frame. These features will be covered in extensive detail in later lessons.

## Utilizing Still Stores

In the Still Store room, you can compare different frames in the Timeline. For example, you may want to perform a before-and-after comparison between an original unmodified shot and its color-corrected version. Or, if the same object appears in two different shots, you may want to compare them to maintain shot-to-shot consistency.

1   At the top of the Composer window, click the Still Store tab.

For this introduction to the Still Store, you'll compare the original shot of the car to one with a Duotone effect applied.

2   Choose Still Store > Store (or press Control-I).

The Timeline frame on which you parked the playhead is saved as a freeze frame, and a thumbnail appears in the Still Store room.

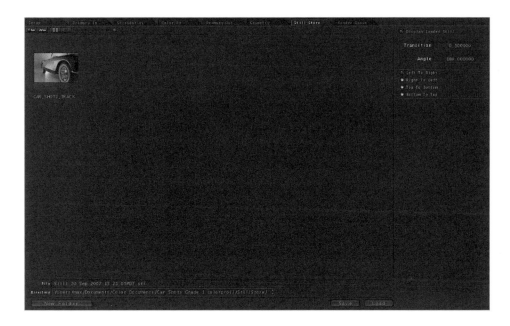

3    At the top of the Still Store, drag the Icon Size slider to adjust the size of the thumbnail.

4    At the top of the Composer window, click the Color FX tab.

5    Double-click the Duotone node to apply it to the image.

The Viewer displays a split screen of the freeze frame from the Still Store and the current frame with the Duotone effect applied.

**NOTE** ▶ If you don't see the split screen, you might have to enable the Still Store by choosing Still Store > Enable (or pressing Control-U).

In the Still Store, you can control the position and direction of the split.

6   Click the Still Store tab.

7   Experiment with the settings in the right side of the window to modify the way that the split screen is drawn.

**TIP** ▶ You can also control the shape and position of the split screen by manually adjusting the Transition and Angle settings.

8   Deselect the Display Loaded Still checkbox (or press Control-U) to disable the split-screen effect in the Viewer.

9   Return to the Color FX room, and delete the Duotone node.

## Correcting the Sequence

So far, you've been introduced to every room except the Render Queue room. But before you render anything, you'll need something to render. In this exercise, you'll use the skills you've learned to correct the three car shots in the sequence, then render your corrections and send the sequence back to Final Cut Pro.

### Correcting Overexposure

The first shot needs some contrast adjustments to improve its overall exposure.

**1** Move your Timeline playhead to the first shot.

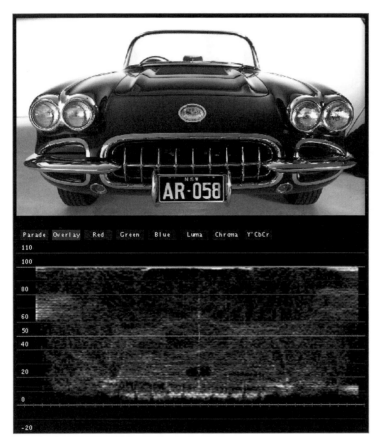

By examining the shot in the Viewer window, you can see that the image is overexposed. White areas are too bright and lack detail, and black areas seem to be dark gray rather than black.

In the Waveform Monitor, the top of the trace is clipped at 100%, indicating that much of the original image is overexposed. While the actual levels shot in the camera likely far exceeded 100%, the Broadcast Safe setting in the Project Settings tab of the Setup room is clipping all levels greater than 100%.

**2** Click the Setup room tab (or press Command-1) and click the Project Settings tab.

**3**   Turn the Broadcast Safe checkbox off and on, and observe the change in the traces in the Waveform Monitor. Be sure to leave it turned off so you can make your corrections manually.

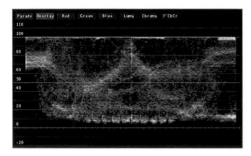
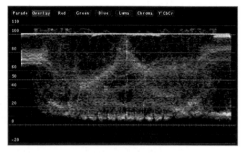

Broadcast Safe Setting On                          Broadcast Safe Setting Off

**4**   Since the image contains black objects, the bottom of the trace should rest at 0%; but since it doesn't, this indicates that the image's black level is not dark enough.

**5**   Click the Primary In tab (or press Command-2).

**6**   While looking at the Waveform Monitor, adjust the Shadow contrast slider so the bottom of the trace rests just at 0%, setting the image's black level at the proper value.

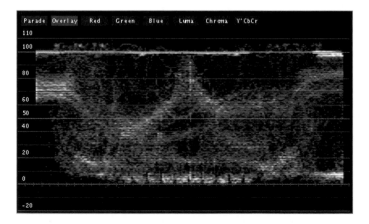

**7**   Adjust the Highlight contrast slider so that the top of the trace is just below 100%, to avoid the clipping caused by the Broadcast Safe filter.

As you lower the level, you'll see more detail in the areas that were previously being clipped. While some areas of this image are pure white, and appear as a solid line, others (such as the area in the headlights and highlights on the hood) have more subtle details that emerge as you lower the level.

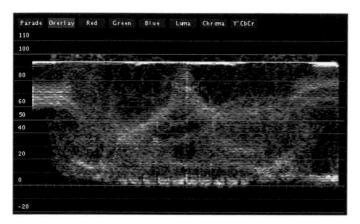

As you grade, you'll frequently want to compare your work with the original image.

**8**   Choose Grade > Disable Grading (or press Control-G).

All color correction adjustments are disabled.

Original                                    Graded

**9**   Press Control-G again to enable the grade and see the improvement that simple white and black level adjustments can make.

Now the headlights have a bit of sparkle, because the glints are brighter than the background cyclorama. If you want to raise the level of the background without pushing the headlight highlights back above the legal limit, you can boost the midtones.

**10** Raise the Midtone contrast slider to increase the white level of the cyclorama by a few points in the Waveform Monitor. Do not push the highlights beyond 100%.

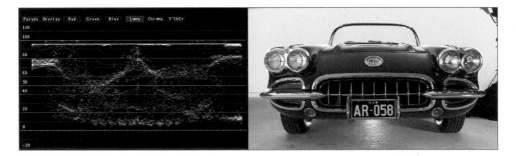

Although this gets the background right, you have now pushed the blacks back up.

**11** Lower the Shadow contrast slider to bring the blacks back down to 0%.

This back and forth is a natural part of color correcting and allows you to fine tune different aspects of your image for optimal grading power.

**12** Press Control-G a few times to turn the grade on and off and see the final results of your work.

### Correcting Underexposure

The next shot in the sequence also needs a contrast adjustment, although in a different direction.

1    In the Timeline, park your playhead on the second shot.

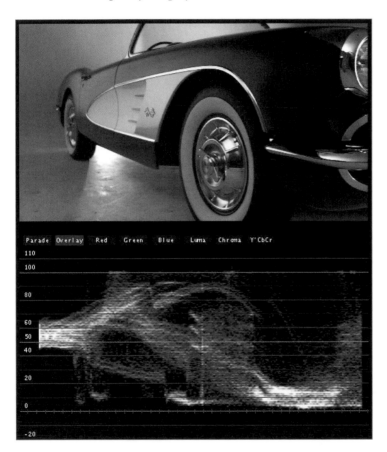

This shot looks too dark. The Waveform Monitor trace shows that the image has proper white and black levels, but most of the trace is low, indicating that the shot is underexposed.

**2** Adjust the Midtone contrast slider to slightly brighten the midtones of the image.

As you make the adjustment, additional details, such as the treads of the tires, emerge in the shadow areas.

You may notice, however, that adjusting the Midtone contrast also affects the white and black points of the image. Although this adjustment helped with the shadow areas, it also overexposed the brightest areas and raised the black level into the gray range.

3   Adjust the Highlight and Shadow contrast sliders to keep the trace between 100% and 0%.

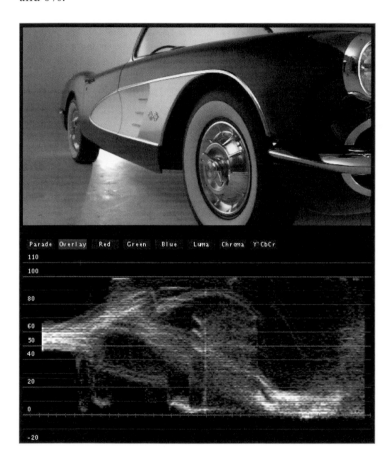

4   Press Control-G to toggle between your corrected shot and the original and assess your changes.

### Correcting Color Casts

The third clip in the sequence has acceptable white and black levels, and the overall brightness appears correct, but the shot has an unwanted yellow color cast. Correcting overall color is also done in the Primary In room.

**1** In the Timeline, park your playhead on the third shot.

The Vectorscope indicates the color shift because much of its trace is pointing toward the yellow overlay. Since the image contains only black and white objects, the trace should be centered to indicate the lack of any specific hue. You can use the color balance controls to correct this unwanted yellow cast.

**2** While watching both the image and the Vectorscope, adjust the crosshair of the Midtone color balance control, dragging it away from the color you want to eliminate (in this case, away from yellow, toward blue) so that the image looks less yellow and the trace is closer to the center of the Vectorscope.

Be careful not to overdo your adjustments, or you may introduce another unwanted color cast.

3   Toggle Control-G to compare your corrected shot with the original.

## Introducing the Render Queue Room

In the Render Queue room, you decide which shots you want to render before returning your sequence to Final Cut Pro.

**1**   At the top of the Composer window, click the Render Queue tab.

In this case, you want to render all three of the car shots but not the green door shot.

**2**   In the Timeline, Shift-click the three car shots to select them.

**3**   At the bottom of the Render Queue room, click the Add Selected button.

Each shot is added to the queue.

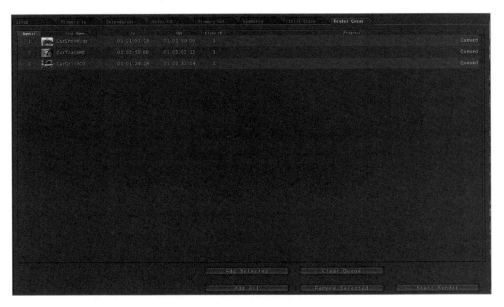

**4**   Click the Start Render button.

As Color renders, it creates new media files on your disk with your rendered corrections. These files are saved in the destination that you specify in the Project Settings tab of the Setup Room.

**5** Once rendering is complete, choose File > Send to > Final Cut Pro.

A dialog appears, warning that not all of your shots have been rendered.

**6** Click Yes.

A second dialog appears informing you that the unrendered clip will be linked to the original media.

**7** Click OK.

Final Cut Pro comes to the foreground, and a new sequence is created with the additional label, *(from Color)*.

**8**   Double-click this sequence to open it.

The color-corrected clips are loaded and your show is ready to output to tape, to Compressor, or the output method of your choice. The round trip between Final Cut Pro and Color is complete.

▶ **Correcting, Timing, and Grading: A Word On the Language of the Colorist**

The task of changing the contrast and color properties of a film or video image has a variety of names that can be somewhat confusing.

While the idea of *correction* implies fixing mistakes, the term color correction is widely used to refer to any work affecting the color, whether it is to correct a mistake, alter the mood, create special effects, or any other related task. However, the overly broad application of the term led to colorists describing all their work as "correcting," which implied that the DPs who shot the material had—in all instances where a colorist intervened—made some kind of mistake.

To help clarify this potential confusion (and protect some egos), some began using the term *color timing* as a way of differentiating elective changes from required fixes, but quickly that term also evolved into a general term for the whole process including correcting mistakes.

The term color timing actually refers to the specific job of determining for how much *time* celluloid film is exposed to different color lights, which has the overall result of controlling the contrast and color attributes of the printed film. Professional color timers resented lowly video engineers calling their work "timing" and so colorists were again stuck with inadequate terminology.

More recently, many have begun using the word *grading* to refer to any color modifcation work, and this is becoming the most popular term today. After all, one colorist's correction is another's elective change.

In this book, we use all three terms—correcting, grading, and timing—somewhat interchangeably. However, with Color, Apple makes a significant differentiation between "corrections," which refer to settings applied in any one room, and "grades," which refer to the combination of effects across multiple rooms.

## Lesson Review

1. In which room are project-specific settings configured?

2. How can you move a sequence from Final Cut Pro to Color?

3. To apply a correction to an isolated portion of an image, which room should be used?

4. What is the difference between the Primary In and Primary Out rooms?

5. What is the difference between a node and a Color FX preset?

6. In which room do you create pan and scan effects?

7. What are the purposes of the three vertical strips located next to the color balance controls?

8. True or false: When making an adjustment to the Highlight contrast slider, the darkest areas of the image are somewhat affected.

9. True or false: The Still Store is where freeze-frame effects are made.

10. How do you choose which clip is affected by the color-correction rooms?

### Answers

1. The Setup room.

2. In Final Cut Pro, choose File > Send to > Color.

3. The Secondaries room.

4. The Primary Out room applies its corrections after the other effects have already been applied.

5. A node is an individual effect module. A Color FX preset is a collection of nodes, prearranged to create a certain effect.

6. In the Geometry room.

7. The three strips are sliders for changing the hue, saturation, and contrast.

8. True.

9. False.

10. In the Timeline, double-click the clip, or position the playhead over that clip.

# 2

| | |
|---|---|
| **Lesson Files** | Color Book Files > Lesson Files > Lesson 02 > Primary Grading.colorproj |
| **Time** | This lesson takes approximately 75 minutes to complete. |
| **Goals** | Familiarize yourself with the Primary rooms |
| | Auto-balance clips, and learn when not to use auto-balancing |
| | Adjust lift, gain, and gamma using contrast sliders |
| | Correct color shifts using color balance controls |
| | Use curves to remove color casts |
| | Set complex curve settings to control contrast |
| | Combine controls to create complex effects |

# Basic Grading

When most people think of color correction, they think of a few common tasks: fixing incorrect white balance or removing an unwanted color cast, matching skin tones in two separate shots, or controlling contrast levels. While, these represent only a sampling of color grading tasks, all of them fall into the category of *primary* color correction. Color can perform all these tasks (and quite a few more) in one of its Primary rooms.

Primary color correction means making changes that affect the entire image—which covers the vast majority of color grading work. Color's Primary rooms (Primary In and Primary Out) contain a variety of controls and tools that facilitate primary corrections with both precision and flexibility.

## Exploring the Primary Room

The Primary room has four main sections. The list area on the left contains saved primary corrections, giving you quick access to settings that you may wish to reuse.

**1** Open Lesson Files > Lesson 02 > **Primary Grading.colorproj**.

**2** Choose File > Reconnect Media and navigate to Lesson Files > Lesson 02 > Media, then click Choose.

**3** Click the Primary In tab or press Command-2 to open the Primary In room.

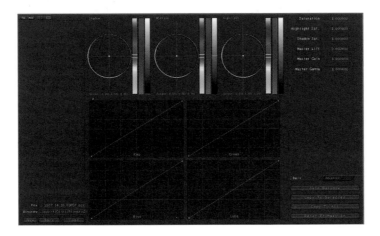

In the upper middle section, you'll find three color balance controls , where you can adjust the shadows, midtones, or highlights of your clip independently. These wheels may be the most versatile and commonly used controls in the entire program. They allow you to modify hue, saturation, and contrast for each range of luma in the image.

These controls are similar to the Color Corrector 3-way in Final Cut Pro. If you already use that filter, you will find this area of the Color interface very familiar.

Color Corrector 3-way in Final Cut Pro

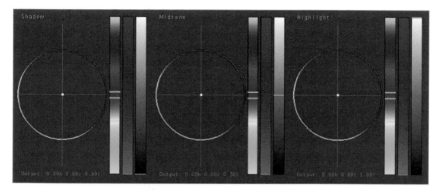

Color balance controls in Color

The black-and-white vertical gradients correspond to the horizontal contrast sliders in Final Cut Pro. The other two gradient strips provide two additional ways to control the position of the target: the hue and saturation sliders.

Below the color balance controls are curve controls for the red, green, and blue luma channels, along with an overall luma channel curve control.

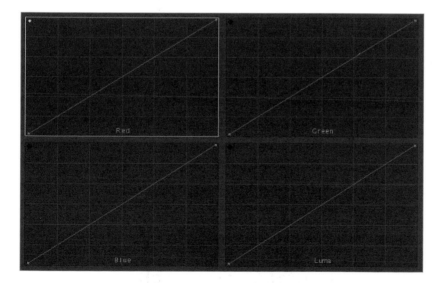

These controls offer more ways to change the overall color of your video based on individual color channels rather than the luma ranges controlled by the color balance controls.

The Luma curve control provides a single control to manipulate the overall luma, allowing you to effectively change the gamma of your image.

To the right of the color balance controls and curve editors you'll find the Saturation panel. While Final Cut Pro's Color Corrector offers a single saturation slider, Color provides more precise and flexible tools for manipulating image saturation.

The Saturation panel includes two tabs: Basic and Advanced. The Basic controls are similar to controls in the color balance control and curve editor sections. The upper three controls perform much like the saturation sliders in the color balance control section, where Saturation controls the midtones, Highlight Sat. controls the highlights, and Shadow Sat. controls the shadows.

The lower three controls are similar to the contrast sliders in the color balance control section. Master Lift works the way the Shadow contrast slider works when Limit Shadow Adjustments is disabled in the User Prefs tab in the Setup room. Master Gain affects the contrast of the highlights (leaving the black point alone), and Master Gamma affects the contrast of the midtones.

These controls let you adjust the parameters more precisely than the other similar controls, and offer the ability to enter a specific numerical value.

The Advanced tab allows you to independently control the lift, gain, and gamma of the red, green, and blue channels. The Printer Point controls here simulate the effect of exposing different colored lights to film in traditional color timing.

As you can see, there is quite a bit of overlap in the different controls in the Primary room, and it is easy to offset the effect of one control by manipulating another. While this may seem confusing, this overlap is actually the key to mastering the art of grading. By applying a strong effect with one control, then offsetting some of the effect with another, you can perform delicate and subtle effects, finessing your images with amazing precision.

## ▶ Where Do I Start?

Beginning colorists are easily overwhelmed by the multiple settings and many methods that are available to modify the look of a shot. While every show and every shot will have different needs, some easy-to-remember guidelines can help simplify your color-grading process.

### Contrast First

As a general rule, set a clip's contrast prior to modifying its color values. While each component of a shot is distinct from the other elements, adjusting one does affect *our perception* of the other.

For example, adjusting a clip's contrast can have a significant impact on its apparent saturation. As the blacks are crushed and highlights whitened, the apparent overall level of saturation increases. Similarly, primary colors tend to appear to have more contrast than complementary colors. Shifting the color balance of a shot from magenta toward red may appear to affect the contrast, even though no change was actually made to the contrast.

If you begin adjusting settings in a haphazard way, you can find yourself chasing your own tail—modifying one setting that only appears to affect another. By consistently setting a clip's black and white point first (and the nature of the gray values between them), you can diminish this effect. Often, correcting a clip's contrast will be the only correction necessary because apparent color issues may disappear when contrast looks correct.

### RGB vs. YUV

As an application, Color operates in a different color space than Final Cut Pro. If you're used to Final Cut Pro, you're used to a YUV (actually YCbCr) color space in which contrast values are stored in a channel that is separate from color values. In a YCbCr space, adjusting the contrast has absolutely no effect on the color; but in RGB, changing the contrast will change the color values, and vice versa. Similarly, in Color, the red, green, and blue channels are truly discrete, so (with rare exceptions) changing red values will have no actual influence on the other channels. (There may be a perceived change, but that's a different issue.)

In Final Cut Pro, stretching contrast (spreading out the white and black levels) tends to result in a perceived *decrease* in saturation (although saturation is mathematically unaffected). In Color, stretching contrast tends to *increase* saturation. This is sometimes a good thing, because it adds color richness at the same time as it increases the contrast, but it is also something to avoid if that added saturation is not intended.

### Trust Your Scopes

Our eyes are easily tricked and easily fatigued. You may think that an image seems overly dark or skewed towards a certain color, but that perception is often just in comparison to another shot, or in comparison to the way the shot looked before you began adjusting it.

The reason Color provides so many scopes and so many ways to view them is to give you something to trust in addition to your own eyes. While it may take you additional time to grow comfortable reading the scopes, they offer an objective view of the exact mathematical values of the pixels in your image. No matter how accurate your grading reference monitor or computer display is, using scopes will always be an essential tool in balancing shots, especially after a long day. Put your trust in them, though ultimately, there is no mechanical substitute for your own eyes.

## Using the Auto Balance Control

Because it's common to begin correcting an image by adjusting its white and black points, Color provides a one-button solution intended to simplify the process. In fact, Color's *auto balance* evaluates the red, green, and blue channels independently, discretely setting the brightest and darkest points of each channel. Often this results in a seemingly magic color correction.

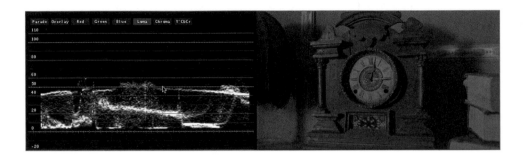

**1** Make sure the first clip (**SHOT02_CLOCK**) is active and click the Auto Balance button (located below the tabs at the bottom of the Saturation panel).

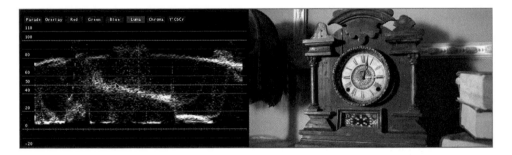

Voilà! The contrast is automatically stretched so the darkest pixel in the frame is set to pure black and the whitest pixel is set to pure white. The image looks almost like a film of grime has been wiped off the screen.

At first glance, Auto Balance may appear to be an amazing fix-it tool that you'll automatically want to apply to all your clips, but there's a catch—several of them, actually.

First, the Auto Balance feature looks only at the current frame. While that frame may look great, other parts of the shot may still need fixing, or may have been negatively affected by that adjustment.

Additionally, if an image has black letterbox margins, as many video clips do, the Auto Balance will see the true black in the margin and won't change the black level in the image, even if it desperately needs it.

**2** Double-click the second clip in the sequence (Letterbox).

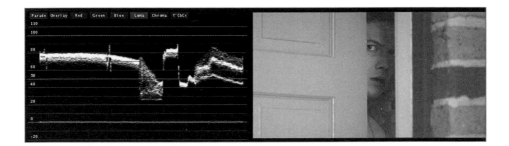

The image is clearly washed out. The Waveform Monitor shows that the contrast needs to be stretched in both directions, but if you look closely, you will see the solid line of trace at exactly 0% indicating the letterbox.

3   In the Primary In room, click the Auto Balance button.

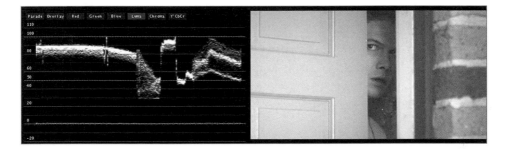

The letterbox fools the Auto Balance control, and the blacks are not adjusted at all. The image still looks washed out and overexposed, although the white levels now have been boosted to exactly 100%.

Auto Balance can make the same mistake for the white levels. If there is a one-pixel highlight in someone's eye or burned-in timecode appears in the clip, Auto Balance will leave the white level unchanged.

Furthermore, while auto balancing may be a quick fix, it is no replacement for manually customizing your contrast. Even the clock shot looked arguably better before the auto balance was applied, stripping it of the pale orange cast that gave the shot its unique period look.

Plus, while Auto Balance does perform a quick-and-easy contrast adjustment, which may be an improvement in many shots, you didn't send your project to Color for quick-and-easy fixes. You came for fine control over every aspect of your images. For that reason, professional colorists almost never use the Auto Balance control.

### Resetting Auto Balance

You may have noticed that when you click the Auto Balance button, none of the controls visible in the Primary In room moved to affect the color change. The controls that are modified when you use Auto Balance are hidden in the Advanced tab.

To remove the effect of the Auto Balance, you need to reset each of the nine number sliders by clicking the cyan dot beside each control.

> **TIP** ▶ You can identify when a number slider has been moved from its default setting because the numbers are drawn in yellow. At the default, they appear white.

Rather than making nine clicks, you can remove the Auto Balance effect by clicking Reset Primary In (below the Auto Balance button). This restores all controls in the Primary In room to their default settings.

## Grading with the Color Balance Controls

The color balance controls allow you to independently manipulate the shadows, midtones, and highlights (called *ranges*) of an image. However, each range has significant overlap (as indicated in the following diagram). Because of this overlap, changing a setting in one range will affect the others, but to a varying extent.

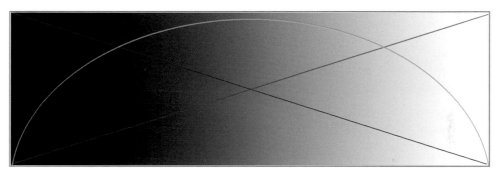

Red: Shadow control influence, Blue: Highlight control influence, Green: Midtone control influence

Furthermore, each range provides specific controls to discretely change the hue, saturation, or contrast.

### Using the Contrast Sliders

Because you'll always begin by adjusting contrast, first you'll explore the contrast controls in each of the ranges. These are the vertical grayscale bars to the right of each color balance control; they are actually sliders in disguise.

1    Double-click the third shot in the sequence (**RHRN_SHOT01_EXTCAR**) to make it the active clip.

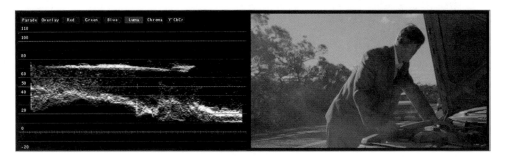

2    Drag the Shadow contrast slider up and down.

Your pointer disappears when you drag, but the darkest areas of the image get darker or brighter. You can also see a cyan line in the slider move up when you drag above the default value.

The Shadow contrast slider has a different effect when you change the Limit Shadow Adjustments setting in the User Prefs tab of the Setup room.

3    Choose Color > Preferences.

The Setup room is brought to the front with the User Prefs tab active.

4    In the upper-right corner of the window, deselect Limit Shadow Adjustments.

5    Press Command-2 to switch back to the Primaries room.

6    Raise the Shadow contrast slider, and observe the Waveform Monitor.

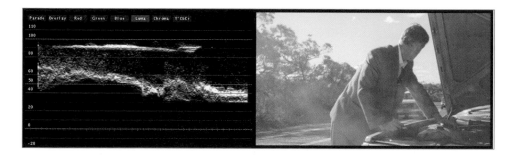

Now, the entire luma moves uniformly up or down as you drag.

7    Press Command-1 to switch back to the Setup room.

8    Click the Limit Shadow Adjustments checkbox to reselect it.

9    Switch back to the Primaries room and move the Shadow contrast slider again.

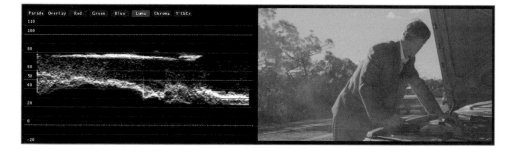

In this setting, dragging the Shadow contrast slider weights the effect toward the shadows.

When the Limit Shadow Adjustment setting is turned off, this effect is called *lift* because it uniformly lifts the overall luma of the image. The other contrast sliders have nifty names too: The Midtone contrast slider adjusts the image's *gamma*, and the Highlight contrast slider adjusts the image's *gain*.

By manipulating an image's lift, gamma, and gain, you can exert precise control over the tonality of your image and correct a variety of exposure problems, as well as cre-ate many different *looks* to support or emphasize the content of the scene.

10   Click the Reset Primary In button in the lower-right corner of the room to remove any miscellaneous changes you may have made.

### Correcting Contrast in a Shot

Proper contrast settings require that the darkest areas of the image be set at true black, and the brightest areas at true white. This is what the Auto Balance setting does, but now you'll do it manually.

**1**   Lower the Shadow contrast slider until the lowest traces on the Waveform Monitor just reach the 0% line.

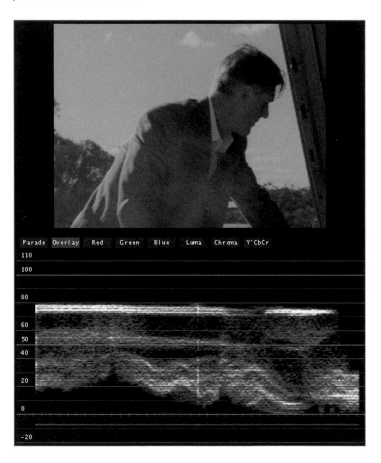

**2**    Raise the Highlight contrast slider until the highest traces in the Waveform Monitor reach 100%.

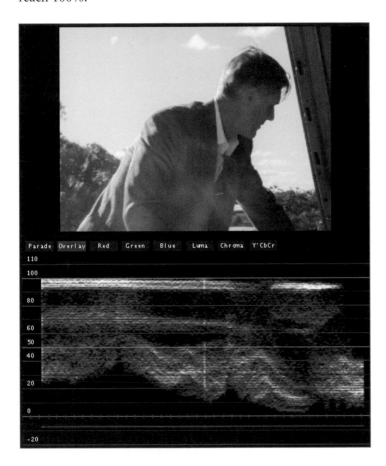

You've manually done what the Auto Balance control does, but this is just the beginning. The blacks are true black and the whites are true white, but the distribution of grays can be adjusted in myriad ways.

**3**    Lower the Midtone contrast slider slightly.

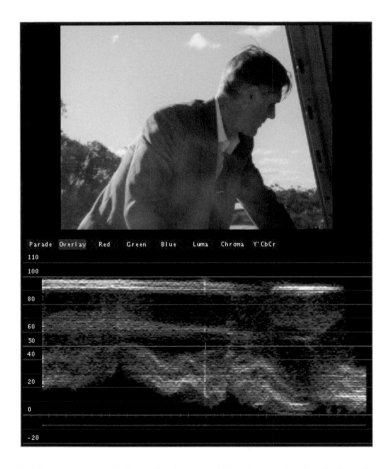

This appears to darken the image giving it a richer look, but doesn't lower the white point, so overall exposure still appears correct.

To reinforce this look, you can *crush* the blacks further, reducing the detail in the darkest shadows, while still leaving the highlights unaffected.

4   Lower the Shadow contrast slider a bit more, until the details disappear in the trees at the lower left.

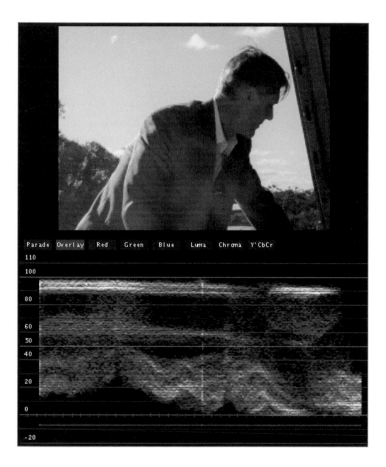

The image now has a good range of contrast levels (the contrast *ratio*), with enough richness in the darks to give it a dramatic, high-contrast look.

### Adjusting Color

When the overall contrast is set to your liking, you can begin modifying the color values. The color balance controls allow you to set the hue and saturation values independently by using the sliders, or you can adjust them at the same time by dragging the handle in the center of the balance control.

While contrast values are most easily viewed in the Waveform Monitor (especially when it is set to monochrome), color values can be viewed in the Vectorscope, or in the Waveform Monitor when it is set to color in the User Prefs tab of the Setup room.

1    Choose Color > Preferences.

This is a quick way to open the User Prefs tab of the Setup room.

2    Deselect the Monochrome Scopes checkbox (just above the Scope Color setting).

This preference changes the view of the scopes in the Viewer so that the traces now appear in the color that corresponds to the channel they represent. In the Waveform Monitor, you'll be able to distinguish between the contrast values of the red, green, and blue channels individually.

You can view the three channels overlaid on each other or you can view them side by side.

3    In the Waveform Monitor, click the Parade button.

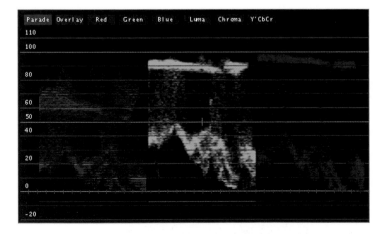

The three color channels' relative chroma values are displayed side by side.

4    In the Waveform Monitor, click the Overlay button.

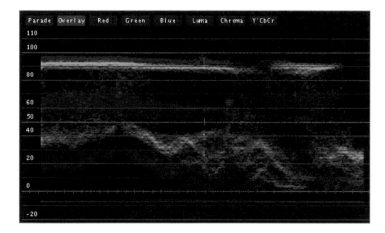

The three waveforms are all displayed over the same graph.

In the Viewer, you can see that this image has a blue-green hue to it. This is reinforced in the Waveform Monitor; the red channel is much lower than the blue and green levels. This makes sense, as the main colors in the shot are the blue sky, the green trees, and the greenish suit the man is wearing.

The Vectorscope also gives you important information about the distribution of colors in the shot. While the large concentration of traces near the cyan target makes sense, given the abundance of sky in the shot, you might also notice that the entire bulk of traces is shifted off-center toward the cyan and green targets.

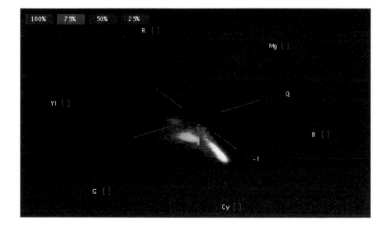

This is a great clue as to how to fix the image.

**5** In the Midtone color balance control, click the handle (the white dot) and drag it around.

As you drag farther from the center point, you add more saturation and the angle you drag toward determines the hue you assign. Adjusting the color balance controls adds a color *influence* to your image. All of the color values in the range you adjust are moved toward that color. This is different from tinting an image when a uniform color cast is added to the image.

**6** Drag the handle away from the green/cyan targets (towards red/magenta) while watching the Vectorscope, and keep dragging until the scope traces are more centered.

As you make this adjustment, you'll see that the whole image begins to improve and look more realistic.

Rather than going further with this one clip, move on to the next clip, which provides similar challenges that you'll solve in a different way.

7   Click anywhere in the Timeline to make it active, then press the Down Arrow key to move to the next clip.

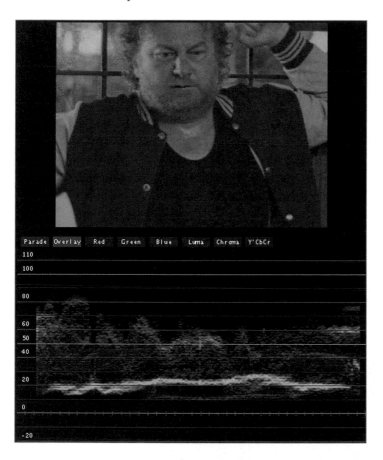

This clip has a cool overall look, which is appropriate for the intense dramatic nature of the scene, so you wouldn't necessarily want to eliminate that. But, the skin tones are a bit too pallid and could use a little warming. Additionally, the contrast is very limited, and should be stretched to give the image more depth and intensity.

8   Starting with the contrast, lower the Shadow contrast until the lowest red traces reach 0% in the Waveform Monitor.

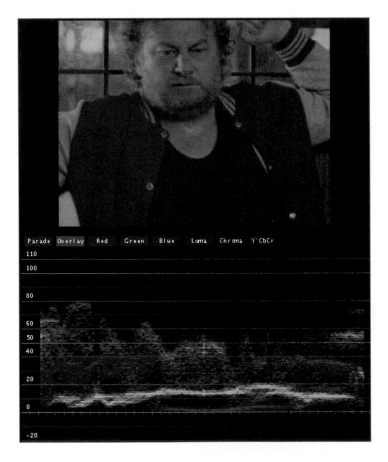

This corrects the black level just like you did with the previous clip.

9   Next, raise the Highlight contrast until the range at the upper left just begins to touch 100% in the Waveform Monitor.

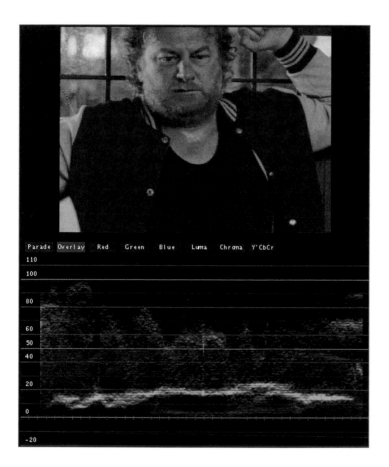

As always, fixing the contrast immediately provides a dramatic improvement to the image. Next you want to warm up the skin tones by adding red-orange to them, but without affecting the rest of the image.

You can do this very quickly right in the Primary In room. The skin tones are mostly in the highlights and midtones of the image, so you can begin by modifying those ranges.

**10** Drag the Midtone color balance control handle slightly toward red/orange (to about 11 o'clock).

**11** Drag the Highlight color balance control handle slightly in the same direction.

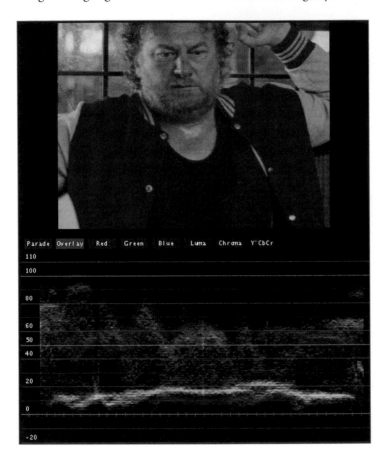

This succeeds in warming up the skin tone, but it also warmed the rest of the image.

One of the secrets of effective color correction is to combine controls to create complex effects. Here, you can use the Shadow color balance control to moderate the effect of the other two ranges.

**12** Drag the Shadow color balance control in the opposite direction (to around 5 o'clock) until the darker areas of the image return to their original cool tones.

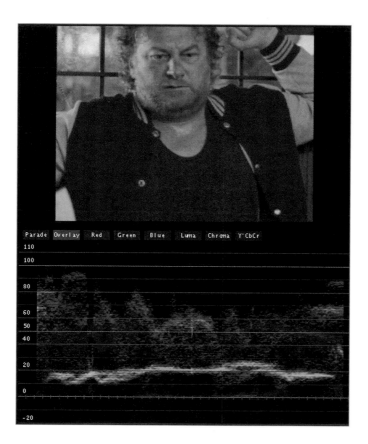

When done right, color correction should be subtle. Small movements can have significant impact, so it's always best to make tiny adjustments until you've achieved the desired result.

It's also nice to recall how far you've come, as you make those many small changes.

**13**  Press Control-G to toggle between the original image and its corrected version.

**14**  Continue making adjustments to the three color balance controls until you are satisfied with the image.

Remember to play the clip occasionally to see how the settings you change affect the whole clip. Later in this clip, the person throwing the money steps into the frame briefly. You may want to stop on one of those frames to ensure that you're happy with the skin tones of that person as well.

### Resetting the Primary Parameters

As you're working in the Primary In room, you may find you've gone too far down one path and you want to start over again. You already know about the reset buttons in the corner of each of the controls, but another control can reset the entire Primary In room.

1   Click the Reset Primary In button, located in the lower-left corner of the Primary In room.

    This restores all the controls in the room to their default values.

2   Before you continue to the next exercise, press Command-Z to Undo the reset, or, for more practice, take a few minutes and re-grade the clip.

## Grading with Curves

Working with the color balance controls is a powerful, flexible, and effective way to grade shots, but it's not the only way. The RGBL curve editors offer a different approach to correcting your clips.

Rather than dividing the image into ranges of brightness, the curves isolate the red, green, blue, and luma channels independently. These controls are ideal for making corrections across the entire contrast range, but along an isolated color. For example, you would use these controls to apply a quick and easy white balance correction to a video clip, or to remove an unwanted color cast.

In the real world, you will use both the color balance controls and the curves in concert, tweaking a variety of settings in both places to achieve the overall look you desire.

Manipulating curves effectively takes some practice and, as with the color balance controls, small curve adjustments can cause big changes in the image.

1   Press the Down Arrow key or click the Timeline ruler area to move the focus to the next clip.

While this clip could benefit from some contrast adjustment, its bigger problem is a slight cyan cast that you'll work to eliminate. To familiarize yourself with the curve editors, you'll correct the cyan cast prior to expanding the contrast, even though in the real world this would not be a typical workflow.

First of all, you must figure out which curve will affect cyan, which means thinking about the color balance control and which primary color opposes it. A quick glance at the Vectorscope (or any of the color balance controls in the Color interface) reveals that cyan and red share the same axis, making them *complementary* colors. So, adjusting the red curve should add or remove cyan from the image.

2   Click in the midpoint of the red curve to create a handle and drag slightly toward the upper-left corner of the graph, adding red, and thereby removing cyan.

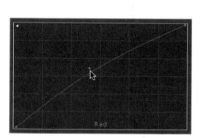 

This reduces the amount of cyan in the image and, because you clicked in the center of the curve, it mostly affects the midtones.

3   Drag the handle you created in step 2 down toward the lower left, so that you're moving only the lower portion of the curve.

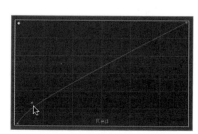 

This limits the cyan reduction to the image shadows. You can see this in the Viewer in the way that the color is pulled out of the suit and the dark background, while the skin tones and white color of the shirt still have a cyan cast.

4   Drag the point to the top of the graph.

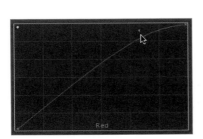

Now the cyan is removed only from the highlights. The shirt and skin tones become more neutral, but the suit and background still have the color cast.

You can also observe how the curves change the image by examining the scopes.

5   Drag the graph handle around as you watch the Waveform Monitor and Vectorscope.

With the Waveform Monitor set to color and overlay mode, it's very clear that only the red channel is affected.

6   Observe how dragging the point near the top of the curve graph limits the effect on the red highlights (the red traces near the top of the Waveform Monitor) and dragging near the bottom limits the effect on the shadows.

7   Keep dragging the handle around, while you watch the Vectorscope.

The red curve moves the entire image along the axis between red and cyan.

8   Drag the blue or green curves and observe the way the traces in the Vectorscope are limited to those other axes.

9   Click the reset button in the upper-left corner of all three curves.

### Controlling Contrast with Curves

In addition to controlling individual colors, you can use a curve editor to modify the luma channel, which controls the overall image contrast.

Changing the Luma curve yields results similar to modifying the contrast sliders in the color balance controls, but the curve editor interface allows different types of corrections and it affects the red, green, and blue luma values all at once.

1   To better monitor the changes you'll be making, click the Luma button at the top of the Waveform Monitor to view just that channel.

2   Click to add a handle in the Luma curve, and drag it toward the bottom of the graph.

Observe the Waveform Monitor to see how the shadows are moved closer to the 0% bar.

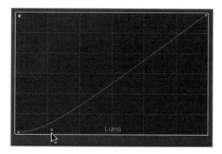

3   Click near the top of the Luma curve to add another handle and, this time, drag it to the left to increase the values near the top.

Observe the Waveform Monitor, dragging until the traces are near the 100% bar.

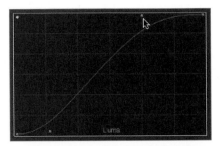

**NOTE** ▶ Dragging the handle outside the graph deletes the point altogether.

Now that you've set the black and white points, you can still make additional changes to the main slope of the curve.

4    Click the middle of the Luma curve and drag a tiny amount toward the upper-left corner until you see some detail emerge in the seat behind the actor.

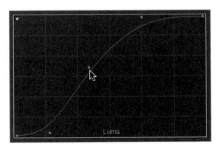

These changes affect the tonality of the image just as the contrast sliders in the color balance controls do, but the curve editor has an advantage because the curve is connected, and you can see how changes in one area impact the other areas.

The overall shape of the Luma curve controls the distribution of gray values across the range of the image, known as the *gamma* of the image. Different recording media, such as film, digital cinema cameras, and video cameras each have different gamma settings that can be simulated using this curve.

## Understanding Additional Controls

The Basic and Advanced tabs at the right of the Primary In window offer several ways to perform the same tasks you performed using the curves and color balance controls.

As you've probably begun to realize, the Primary In room provides many ways to apply the same types of effects. Some colorists may gravitate toward the balance controls or the curves, and old-school film color timers might be more comfortable using the printer point controls in the Advanced tab. There is no right or wrong way to employ these different tools.

One distinguishing element of the controls in the Basic and Advanced tabs is that they allow precise numerical entry, so you can quickly make relative adjustments—lowering a value by a set amount, or exactly matching the values across multiple clips.

While you can always type a number directly into these fields, Color also allows you to treat these controls as virtual sliders. When your pointer is positioned over any of these fields, rolling your mouse scroll wheel will raise or lower the values. Alternatively, you can middle-click and drag the slider left or right to set the value lower or higher.

**1** With the Timeline active, press the Down Arrow key to move to the next clip (**10_OLDPLANES**).

This shot needs some contrast adjustment, as well as some minor color work. First is to set the black and white points.

**2** In the Basic tab of the Primary In room, middle-click the Master Lift value and drag left. Watch the Waveform Monitor, and darken the image until the shadows are just approaching 0%.

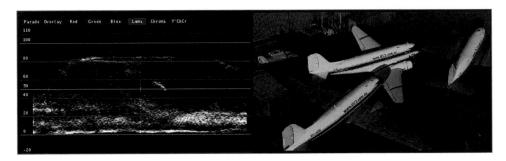

This sets the approximate black point.

**3** Middle-click the Master Gain control and drag right until the Waveform Monitor shows the white levels nearing 100%.

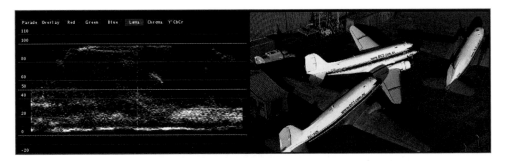

This sets the white point, but the image can still use some color adjustments. The airplanes appear very yellow, making them look dirty and old. Rather than use the curves or color balance controls to offset the yellow, you can use the saturation sliders to remove all color from the brightest highlights in the image.

**4** Middle-click the Highlight Sat. control and drag left to remove saturation from the highlights. Watch the image in the Viewer and stop dragging when the planes appear clean and white (at approximately .25).

The Shadow Sat. slider also can be used to quickly remove a color cast from the shadows of an image, giving the blacks a more *inky* look. The 3D Color Space scope can be a great aid in performing this sort of correction.

**5** If the 3D Color Space scope is not already showing, right-click (or Control-click) the Vectorscope and choose 3D Color Space to enable that scope.

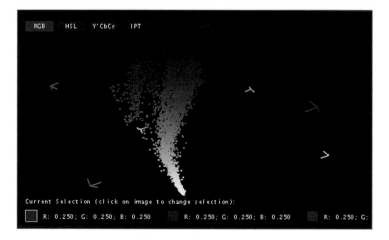

The 3D Color Space scope is like a Vectorscope extruded into three dimensions along the axis of luma; so in addition to the six color targets, there are also targets for black and white, indicating the contrast of the image. To make it even easier to read, the traces are colored (even when the monochrome scopes setting is enabled).

**TIP** ▶  You can also view this scope in different color spaces by clicking the buttons above the graph.

6   Drag around in the scope to rotate it until the black is on the top and the red is on the left (as illustrated in the figure above).

In this image, you can see that a fair number of red traces are present in the shadow area of the scope and they are far from the center axis. This indicates that the shadows have some saturated red color.

7   Middle-click the Shadow Sat. control and drag to the left to decrease saturation in the shadows. Watch the 3D Color Space scope as you drag.

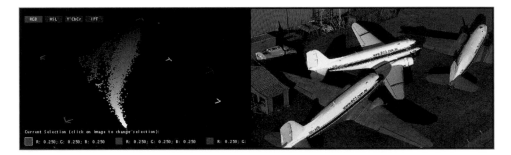

8   The red traces near the black point draw close to the middle axis, and in the viewer, you can observe the shadows become more monochromatic.

The Primary In room is incredibly versatile and you will undoubtedly find yourself employing the controls in many situations. Because each of the controls (color balance controls, curves, number sliders, and so on) affects the picture differently, you can exercise your artistry by combining and overlapping them in unique and unexpected ways.

# Lesson Review

1.  True or false: The Primary rooms are only for changing primary colors.
2.  How do the sliders to the right of the color balance controls affect the color balance control itself?
3.  Identify three situations when auto balance is likely to produce undesirable results.
4.  How do you remove the effect of the Auto Balance command?
5.  Do colorists typically correct color or contrast first?
6.  How do you configure monochrome scopes to display color data?
7.  How does the Primary Out room differ from the Primary In?
8.  Can curves contain multiple control points?
9.  How are the curve editors different from the color balance controls?
10. How do you change the value of the numerical fields in the Basic tab?

*Answers*

1.  False. Primary corrections affect the entire image.
2.  The hue slider controls the angle, the saturation slider controls the distance from the center, and the contrast slider has no visible effect on the balance control, but affects the black and white levels for that brightness range.
3.  Letterboxed clips, BITC clips, and clips in which the content changes significantly across the duration of the clip.
4.  Click the Reset Primary In button.
5.  Contrast is usually corrected first.
6.  Deselect the Monochrome scopes setting in the Setup room's User Prefs tab.
7.  Primary Out changes are applied after secondaries.
8.  Yes.
9.  Curves affect color channels and color balance controls affect brightness ranges.
10. Type a number in, or position the mouse pointer over the field and rotate the mouse scroll balance control.

# 3

**Lesson Files**   Color Book Files > Lesson Files > Lesson 03 > Secondaries.colorproj

**Time**   This lesson takes approximately 75 minutes to complete.

**Goals**   Master the concept of secondary corrections

Isolate specific colors for corrections using the eyedropper and HSL qualifiers

Mask discrete sections of an image using simple shapes called vignettes

Control the inside and outside of a vignette independently

Use curves to limit corrections to a specific hue

# Basic Secondary Grading

Whereas adjustments made in the Primary rooms affect the entire image, often you want to modify a portion of the frame discretely. For example, you may want to adjust human skin tones; or if you're working with an image shot outdoors, you may need to make color adjustments to the sky. Perhaps you want to add some saturation to the blues while removing some from the reds. Furthermore, you may want to employ masks to limit corrections to a certain shape or object within the frame. Any changes that affect a limited section of the shot are considered *secondary* corrections, and so are done in the Secondaries room of Color.

While primary corrections are typically used to correct exposure and color balance problems, or to match the overall appearance of your shots, secondaries are where you can define a unique *look* for your shots, and where you can do the detailed finessing that colorists relish.

Because secondaries modify limited portions of the frame, it is common to employ many of them in the same shot.

For example, in the image above, the sky, bushes, human skin, and sand each have individual corrections applied to them. Color's Secondaries room has eight tabs allowing you to perform eight different corrections simultaneously. When you take into account the ability to control the inside and outside of vignettes, this allows for 16 independent secondary controls. So you will never run out of secondaries.

## Three Types of Secondaries

There are three different types of secondary corrections performed in the Secondaries room: *key-based* corrections, *vignette-based* corrections, and *curve-based* corrections.

### Key-Based

Key-based corrections are controlled by selecting a range of color using the HSL qualifiers—hue, saturation, and lightness sliders—in the upper-right corner of the Secondaries room.

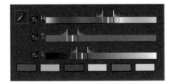

**TIP** ▶ You can also use the eyedropper or color swatches to select the desired color.

This is called *key-based correcting*, because it works the same way as traditional bluescreen or greenscreen color keying. These sorts of secondaries are perfect for working on sections that fall in a continuous range of color, such as skies, skin tones, and other color-based selections, regardless of whether they appear contiguously within the image. But most secondary color-correction keys do not necessitate the level of precision or accuracy required by keying for compositing.

> **NOTE ▶** Key-based corrections work the same way as the Limit Effect controls in Final Cut Pro's Color Corrector 3-way.

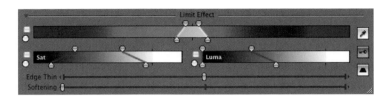

Once you've identified the color you want to modify, any changes made in the color balance controls will apply only to that selected color.

### Vignette-Based

You employ vignette-based secondaries when the area of the frame you want to limit is not based on a color, but rather on a shape. You may want to use a simple circle or rectangle, or you may draw a custom shape in the Geometry room. Such shapes can encompass a range of colors, and you can even combine multiple noncontiguous shapes to create complex and powerful masks.

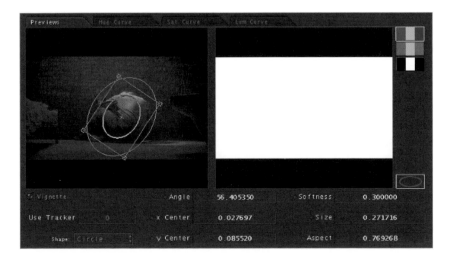

Once a mask has been created, changes made in the color balance controls will affect only the area within (or outside of) that isolated region.

> **TIP** ▶ Masks and keys can be combined in the same secondary to create a selection based on a combination of color and shape.

### Curve-Based

Another way to apply an effect to a limited section of your image is to use the secondary hue, saturation, and luma curves in the center of the Secondaries room.

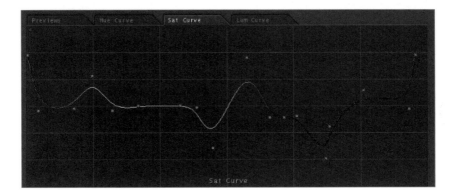

While these curves resemble the curves in the Primary rooms, and you manipulate them in a similar way, the secondary curves are used in a very different way.

The spectrum displayed on the length of the curves allows you to make hue, saturation, and luma adjustments to a limited range of that spectrum.

## Performing Key-Based Secondaries

One common type of secondary correction is based on identifying a specific color and applying a correction to just that color.

1   Open Lesson Files > Lesson 03 > **Secondaries.colorproj**.

2   Choose File > Reconnect Media, navigate to Lesson Files > Lesson 03 > Media, and click Choose.

Your Timeline playhead should be parked on the first clip, the overhead shot of the stadium. This clip has already had some primary color correction applied to stretch out the contrast, but the green grass field looks dark and ugly. This is a perfect example of a situation where a secondary correction can bring some life back to a part of an image.

**3**    Click the Secondaries tab.

**4**    Select the Enabled checkbox at the top of the window.

**NOTE ▶** Setting this checkbox is required to activate the controls in the Secondaries room, but it's so small and out of the way that it's easily forgotten. Clicking the eyedropper activates this automatically, but it's good practice to turn it on manually whenever you're beginning a secondary correction. It's often useful to turn these on and off to quickly show directors or producers the subtle changes that have been made.

**5**    Click the eyedropper in the upper-right section of the Secondaries room.

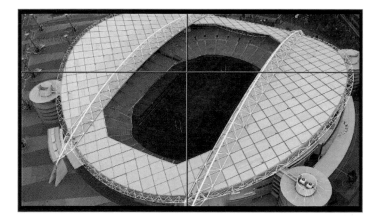

A red crosshair appears in the Viewer. Your next click will establish the color that you will isolate for the secondary effect. But before you click, you can increase the range of colors to be keyed by dragging across the colors in the image.

**6** Drag the red crosshair across the football field.

The color of the field is selected, and now any changes you make to the color balance controls will be limited to that selection.

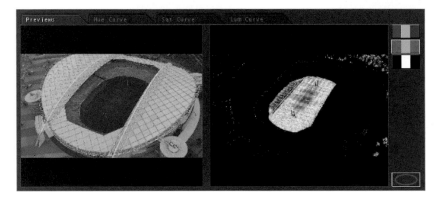

In the Previews tab in the center of the Secondaries room, the key is displayed as a white selection in a field of black. The Matte Preview Mode buttons to the right of the matte view control the display in the Viewer.

By default, the middle button (gray-green-gray), which displays the selection in color, is active, and the rest of the image is in grayscale.

**7** Click the black-white-black button to set the Viewer to display the mask only.

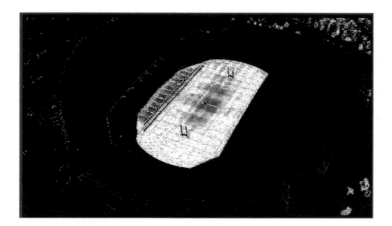

This provides a larger and more detailed view of the masked area in the Viewer.

Depending on exactly how you dragged to select the green field, other unwanted areas of the image may also have been selected. In the image above, you can see some white areas in the lower-left and upper-right corners of the image. These areas will be affected by any corrections you make, which is undesirable in this case.

While it's not essential to get a "perfect" key in order to make a great secondary, you can tidy up the key using the HSL sliders beneath the eyedropper. The goal is to make the area you want to select appear white, while the area you don't want should be black. Areas that appear in gray will be semi-transparent.

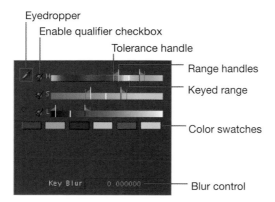

The areas between the handles indicate the hue, saturation level, and brightness level to be keyed.

You can drag the area between the handles to select a new range. Dragging a handle allows you to shrink or expand the selected range symmetrically, and Shift-dragging moves one handle without affecting the other. The outside edge of each handle defines its tolerance, allowing you to taper off the effect gradually.

**8** Shift-click the left range handle of the Hue slider and drag it to the right until the white specks outside of the stadium disappear, but stop before the grassy area itself begins to disappear.

 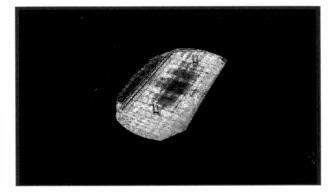

**9** Drag the Lightness range handles closer together until they're nearly touching, and then drag the tolerance handles and soften the selection.

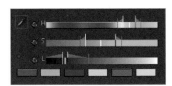

**NOTE ▶** Depending on the specific selection you made in step 5, you may need to make slightly different adjustments to create the optimal key.

**10** Middle-click the Key Blur number slider and drag to the right to about .75. If you don't have a three-button mouse (even though the software requires it), type in .75.

**NOTE ▶** Remember, keying for color correction is very different from pulling a key for compositing. By softening the key, you ensure that the effects you make will blend better into the surrounding image. If you over-soften, you will notice a halo around the selected area.

**TIP** ▶ In general, you can expect to use a blur around 1 to 2 for HD or high-resolution film scanned images. For lower resolutions or very grainy footage, you may need to use a setting of 2 to 4. Note that the maximum value is 8.

Now that you've effectively isolated the field, you're ready to enhance its color.

**11** Click the Final Image display button (red-green-blue) to the right of the matte in the Previews tab.

— Final Image
— Desaturated Preview
— Matte Only

This sets your Viewer to display the final corrected output.

**12** Drag the Shadow contrast slider up slightly.

**13** Drag the Midtone color balance control handle toward yellow-green (about 8 o'clock) until the field takes on a nice, healthy, fresh-grass look.

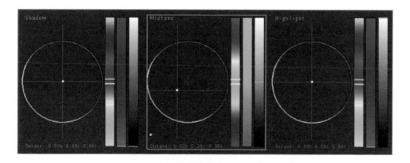

As you make these adjustments, you can see the green traces begin to separate from the center blob in the Vectorscope. While the area in your selection grows greener, notice that the rest of the image remains unaffected.

This sort of keyed secondary is highly effective on skin tones, skies, or any other element that can be isolated by its color values.

## Keying with HSL Qualifiers

In some cases, the eyedropper is not the best way to select the range of color you want to isolate. For example, you may want to select an area of your image based only on its brightness, or only the saturation level.

This can also aid in keying highly compressed footage, such as HDV. Such footage discards far more color (chroma) data than it does luma, so if you want to key based on a color, you're likely to get jagged edges; but if you key based only on the lightness, you can achieve a much smoother edge.

Of course, as stated earlier, keying for secondary color correction rarely requires such a perfect smooth edge, but there are still cases where you may want to key using the hue, saturation, and lightness qualifiers independently.

1   In the Timeline, press the Down Arrow key to move to the next shot (**Shot04_BOAT**).

The water in this shot falls into a fairly narrow hue and saturation range, but the luma variance gives it some depth. You can key a narrow band of the luma to add some color and change the tone of the shot.

**2**  In the Secondaries room, select the Enable checkbox.

**3**  Deselect the checkboxes for hue and saturation, and leave the lightness qualifier selected.

**4**  Shift-drag the left range of the lightness slider to asymmetrically limit the lightness range until the matte in the preview area clearly defines only the lightest portion of the image.

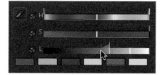

**5**  Shift-drag the tolerance handle to soften the left side of the qualifier.

**6**  Middle-click the Key Blur setting and drag to soften the overall key slightly. Approximately 2.0 to 2.5 is appropriate for this footage.

**7**  Drag the Highlight color balance control toward cyan to give the water a blue-green color.

Now the water looks as if it's in a tropical reef.

## Performing Vignette-Based Secondaries

While keying is great for some footage, often a simple shape will do. When you want to add a gradient of color to enhance a sky or add a pool of light (or shadow) to an image to provide depth, Color's vignettes allow you to limit a correction to the area inside or outside a designated shape.

Just as with keying, you begin by isolating an area of the screen, and then make changes to the color balance controls to perform corrections on the isolated area. Also, just as with keying, the goal is usually not about achieving a level of fine precision, but rather to perform subtle enhancements.

1   With the Timeline active, press the Down Arrow key to move to the next clip (**03_HARBORTRACK**).

This is a dull scenic shot of Sydney harbor with flat exposure. However, with a bit of secondary correction, you can turn it into a masterpiece.

2   Click the Secondaries tab, if it's not already active, to bring that room to the front.

3   Select the Enable checkbox to turn on the Secondary.

Color's vignettes are controlled by the settings beneath the Previews tab or graphically in the Previews tab.

**4**  Click the Vignette button to enable the vignette effect.

A circle appears in the preview area.

For this example, you'll begin by adding some color to the sky using a rectangular vignette.

**5**  Click the Shape pop-up menu and choose Square.

The shape in the preview area turns into a square.

You can manipulate the shape directly in the preview area.

**6**  Click any corner of the square and drag it outward to enlarge the shape until it becomes a rectangle the size of the sky.

**TIP**  Pressing Shift as you scale the shape will constrain the proportions.

**7**   Click anywhere in the middle of the shape to move it up so that it covers the sky.

**8**   Middle-click anywhere on the shape and drag to soften its edges.

The softness is represented by inner and outer boxes around the shape that indicate the falloff range of the softness. The farther away from the original shape, the softer the edge of the effect.

**NOTE ▶** Softness plays an important role when you need to disguise a mask. With moving shots, it's vital to not make masked corrections obvious to the viewer initially.

**TIP ▶** You can continue manipulating the shape at this point, but be careful to drag the corners of the actual shape, not the boxes representing the softness.

**9**   Position the shape so that the bottom softness edge lines up with the horizon line.

Now that the shape is positioned, you can begin to make color adjustments.

**10**   Drag the Midtone color balance control toward blue.

The sky color gets deeper and richer.

**NOTE ▶** You won't see the effect in the preview area. To see the results of your adjustments, watch the Viewer window.

**11**   Toggle Control-G on and off to see a quick before and after of the change you made.

### Controlling Both Sides of the Vignette

Defining a shape doesn't mean your corrections must be limited to the area within it. For every secondary correction, you actually have two sets of settings: inside and outside. Both are active all the time.

Often, making changes within a selection will compel you to make corresponding changes outside it. For example, adding a lighting effect generally requires lightening the inside area and darkening the area around it. Similarly, in the harbor shot, once you create a grade for the sky, you can quickly and easily set a grade for the water using the same mask.

1 Set the Control pop-up menu (above the Highlight color balance control) to Outside.

The blue color you added to the sky remains, but now any changes you make will be applied to the area outside the mask.

2 Drag the Midtone color balance control toward the green/cyan (around 6 to 7 o'clock).

This adds a nice tropical color to the water.

Once you've defined the basic looks for both inside and outside, you may find you want to make additional adjustments to the vignette shape or position.

3   In the preview area, drag the vignette up or down to finesse the location of the transition from sky to water.

4   If necessary, middle-click and drag the Softness control to adjust the softness of the mask edge.

5   Press Control-G to toggle the grade on and off to see how far you've come.

With this one simple mask and a couple of quick adjustments, you've transformed this drab shot into something much more pleasing.

## Creating a Look

While primary correction is commonly used to balance your shots and bring everything into the same overall palette and tone, secondaries are employed to add more specific and unique looks to individual shots. You might say that this is where you add a little "love" to your shots.

For example, if you wanted to make the harbor shot look as if it had been taken at sunrise, you would need only to make a few minor adjustments to the secondary you've already created.

Because the Outside correction is currently selected, you can begin there.

1   Click the reset button for the Midtone color balance control.

2   Drag the Midtone color balance control toward blue (around 3 to 4 o'clock) to give the water a darker, richer color.

3   Drag the Shadow contrast slider down to darken the shadows in the water until the traces in the Waveform Monitor approach 10%.

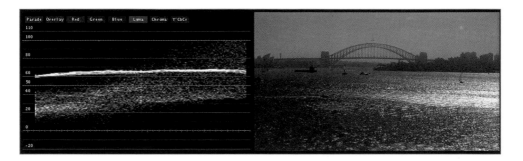

This gives the water the right look, but the highlights on it are a bit tricky. Rather than trying to correct them out, it's better to work with what your footage gives you. If you adjust the mask position to simulate the sun coming from that direction, you can leave the highlights alone.

**4**   In the preview area, move the mask so that you can drag one of the corners.

Remember you can manipulate only the vignette itself, not the boxes representing the softness drop-off zones.

**5**   Right-click (or Control-click) one of the corners to rotate the mask about −7 degrees clockwise; then position the mask over the upper-right corner of the image.

**TIP** ▶ Alternatively, you can middle-click and drag the Angle control; however, by default this slider moves in tiny increments, so to magnify your adjustment, hold down Option as you drag with the middle button.

**6**   Middle-click and drag the mask in the preview area (or the Softness control) to increase the softness significantly (around .75).

**7**   Set the Control pop-up menu to Inside.

**8**   Reset the Midtone color balance control.

**9**   Drag the Highlight contrast slider up until the right side of the thick line in the Waveform Monitor that represents the sky reaches about 90%.

**10**   Drag the Highlight color balance control toward red (or magenta or orange, depending on your preference) to add some morning color to the sky.

You will probably want to continue adjusting the vignette position as well as the corrections applied to the inside and outside until you're satisfied with the effect. One obvious improvement might be to add a little pink to the reflection in the water.

**11**   Set the Control pop-up menu back to Outside.

**12**   Increase the Highlight saturation slightly to add a touch of color to the water reflections.

**NOTE** ▶ If in step 10 you made your sky orange or magenta (instead of red), you might need to adjust the angle of the outside Highlight hue to match that color.

**13** Press Control-G to toggle the grade on and off.

This illustrates the power of using secondaries to create seemingly complex effects with a minimum of steps.

## Secondary Curves

The Secondaries room also contains a set of curves to enable hue, saturation, and luma adjustments based on specific hue values in your source image. For example, this allows you to boost the saturation of red while simultaneously removing it from green. You might use these curves to alter the hue of a single color range, turning all the blue areas to green without affecting any other colors.

These curves are popular controls among colorists partly because they're just fun to use.

**1** In the Timeline, double-click the last clip (**01_JAIL**) to activate it for grading.

2   In the Secondaries room, select the Enable checkbox.

3   Click the Sat Curve tab.

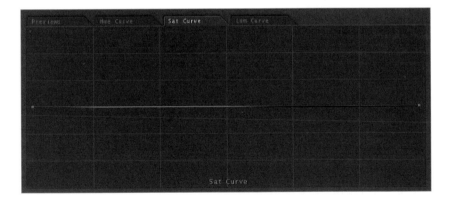

You manipulate these curves the same way as you do the ones in the Primary In room—by clicking to add control points (handles) and dragging the handles to new positions to perform the effect. The Sat curve controls the image's saturation; dragging up adds saturation and dragging down removes it.

The spectrum displayed on the curve indicates which parts of the curve affect which colors. Dragging the red section of the curve will limit the change to that color. You can control the amount of falloff by adding additional adjacent points.

In this example, you will begin by removing saturation from the yellow-green wall and floor.

**TIP** ▶ Often it's practical to add several points to the line before adjusting any of them.

4   Add four points to the curve, two around yellow and two around cyan.

5   Drag the two inner points down until the wall becomes desaturated.

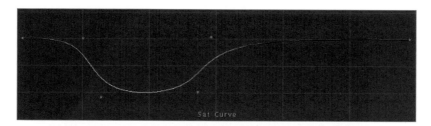

You may want to adjust the adjacent handles to increase or decrease the angle of the falloff.

Now you can add saturation to the orange jumpsuit using the same control.

**6**  Add two new points, one directly on orange, and one to the right of it, to limit the effect.

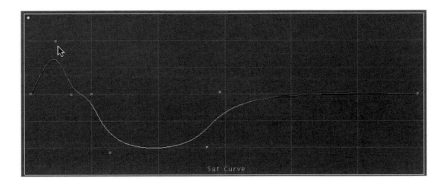

**7**  Drag the orange point upward to increase the saturation of that color.

This image doesn't have much that falls between the two areas you've changed, but if you want to level off the area between the two sections, you can adjust the adjacent points or add a new point.

**8** Add another point directly on yellow and adjust it to create a flat area between the boosted orange and the attenuated green.

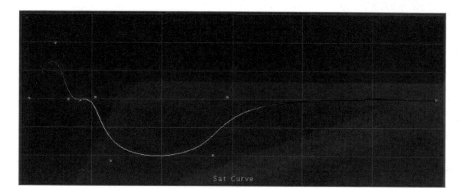

**9** Press Control-G to toggle the grade on and off to see the results of your work.

**TIP** ▶ The curves wrap around, so adjusting the red on one side of the graph will affect the other side of the curve.

### Changing Hue with the Secondary Hue Curve

Similar to changing saturation using the secondary Sat curve, the Hue curve allows you to change the color of a limited portion of the spectrum.

**1** Click the reset button in the upper-left corner of the Sat Curve tab.

**2** Click the Hue Curve tab.

**3** Add three points to the curve in the red orange area. (The built-in point on the left edge serves as your fourth point.)

Don't worry about making their positions precise.

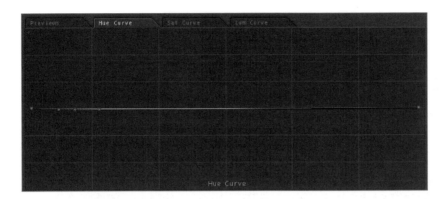

**4**   Drag the second point up to turn the orange elements in the shot purple.

**NOTE ▶** You may have to move your point left or right to ensure that it affects the orange jumpsuit.

**5**   Drag the third point left or right until the entire jumpsuit is affected by the hue shift.

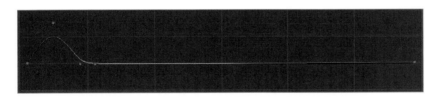

At this stage, you could continue making adjustments to change the hues of other colors within the shot.

These curves are easy to use and allow you to make quick, simple adjustments to various aspects of the shot based on hue. They are not ideal for every situation, but they can be very effective with shots that have clearly contrasting ranges of color.

The third curve, the Lum curve, works exactly the same as the Hue and Sat curves and makes it just as easy to adjust the image. However, it's very easy to tear apart your image by making even modest adjustments with any of these curves, so many colorists choose to make such changes using the controls in the Primary In room or using the keying tools in the Secondaries room.

> **TIP** ▶ The curves are not limited by key- or vignette-based selections. They will always affect the entire image (limited only by the specific points on the curve).

Secondary corrections are incredibly versatile and powerful. Now that you've gotten the hang of how to use the various controls in this room, the next lesson will teach you how to combine them for even more varied and unique effects.

## Lesson Review

1. What is a secondary correction?
2. What are the three main secondary controls?
3. What are the three matte preview modes and where are they selected?
4. How is a key color most often selected?
5. How is the falloff range set in the HSL qualifiers?
6. How is a vignette shape enabled?
7. Where is the vignette shape modified?
8. How do you soften the edge of a vignette?
9. True or false: Changing the Control pop-up menu from Inside to Outside resets your Inside settings.
10. Why are the Hue, Sat, and Lum curves considered secondary corrections?
11. True or false: The Sat curve allows you to change an image's saturation based on hue.
12. On what parameter does the Hue curve base its changes?

*Answers*

1.  A correction that is limited to an isolated portion of the image.

2.  Key based, vignette (mask) based, and curve based.

3.  Final Image, Desaturated Preview, and Matte Only; choose one of the three colored buttons at the right of the Previews tab.

4.  Click the eyedropper and click or drag across a color in the Viewer window.

5.  Drag just outside the qualifier handles to soften the selection.

6.  Select the Vignette checkbox below the preview area on the Previews tab.

7.  Change the vignette shape in the preview area.

8.  Drag the shape with the middle mouse button in the preview area, or adjust the Softness slider in the Vignette controls section.

9.  False. You can have both Inside and Outside settings simultaneously.

10. Because they affect only one portion of the image at a time.

11. True.

12. Hue.

# 4

**Lesson Files**  Color Book Files > Lesson Files > Lesson 04 > AdvancedSecs.colorproj

**Time**  This lesson takes approximately 75 minutes to complete.

**Goals**  Apply multiple secondaries to create complex corrections

Further master key-based, vignette-based, and curve-based secondaries

Combine a key and a vignette in one secondary

Combine two keys in a single shot

Create custom-shaped masks

Adjust softness and other parameters of user shapes

Combine multiple vignettes in a single shot

Apply curve-based corrections to shots with existing secondaries

# Advanced Secondary Grading

Once you master the various tools in the Secondaries room, you can begin to combine them to create an even greater range of effects and corrections. In fact, if you have a shot that requires secondary work, it's very likely you'll want to do more than one secondary. Major feature film colorists employ many secondaries on every single shot; they'll finesse skin tones (often independently for each character), tweak skies, and use other aspects of color and tone to control the audience's point of focus at every moment. There's no reason you can't put the same effort into your own work—and depending on your clients, you may be required to!

Secondaries can be combined in any way imaginable: You can employ multiple keys to treat distinct colors differently; isolate a specific region based on color, and further limit that region based on a vignette; incorporate multiple vignettes; and so on, all the while using the curves to further manipulate specific hues.

Additionally, in Lesson 3, the vignettes you used were limited to simple shapes, but with Color you can create custom shapes with a tremendous amount of flexibility, allowing you to isolate even challenging or complex regions. In this lesson, you'll learn how.

## Using Multiple Secondaries

All this combining of effects can be done in multiple ways. Within the Secondaries room, you can employ curves, keys, and vignettes simultaneously. A range of color selected with a key can be extended or limited by enabling the vignette controls. The settings of the color balance controls will be applied to the combined selection (both inside and outside). The curves work simultaneously, ignoring the selection defined by the key and vignette settings, but limited by the points you set on the curve.

Furthermore, the Secondaries room contains eight tabs along the bottom, each one containing the full set of secondaries controls. This means you effectively have eight different Secondaries rooms for each clip, each one capable of all the complex effects described above. Plus each room has both an inside and an outside setting (for affecting the area within the key or vignette as well as the area outside of it).

## Combining a Key and a Vignette

One very practical way to combine secondaries is to select a region of color using a key, and then limit that selection using a vignette. This is common in shots where the color you want to isolate appears in several objects within the frame. For example, you might use this technique to correct different characters' faces independently.

### Pulling the Key

In this exercise, you'll use a vignette to correct the tone of a character's face while not affecting the similarly colored brick wall.

1    Open Lesson Files > Lesson 04 > **AdvancedSecs.colorproj**.

2    Choose File > Reconnect Media and navigate to Lesson Files > Lesson 04 > Media, then click Choose.

The first clip in the project is the shot you manipulated in Lesson 1 of the man peeking out from behind a green door.

The man is not visible in the initial frame, so first you must find a frame that shows the man's face.

3   Play the clip (by pressing the spacebar or L) until the door is open and the face is exposed. (This happens around frame 8:05, as displayed in the Current Frame field to the right of the Timeline ruler.)

4   Click the Secondaries tab (or press Command-3) to open the Secondaries room.

5   Click the Preview tab in the center of the window if it is not already showing.

**6**   Click the Desaturated Preview button (gray-green-gray).

**7**   Click the eyedropper, and in the Viewer, drag the red crosshairs across the man's forehead and cheek until the entire face appears in color.

Although the face is easily selected, you'll notice that the brick wall contains many of the exact same colors, so that gets selected automatically as well.

Don't worry about the brick, but you will need to adjust the key to deselect the area under the man's chin and further finesse the selection.

**8**   Shift-click the left range handle of the Lightness qualifier control and drag to the right until the area beneath the man's chin turns mostly black in the Preview area.

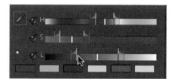

**NOTE** ▶ If you begin to remove the shadowed portion of the man's face, increase the tolerance handles (the outer lines) in the Lightness qualifier control to split the difference.

9   Drag the Saturation qualifier range handles slightly closer together to remove some additional white from that area.

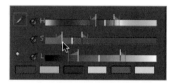

10   Middle-click the Key Blur number slider and drag to the right to increase the blur to about .75.

**TIP** ▶ For color correction purposes, it's not essential to pull a perfect key.

### Adding the Vignette

Now that you've got the face pretty well isolated, it's time to take care of that brick wall that has been accidentally selected.

**1**   Click the Vignette button in the vignette area beneath the preview area.

**2**   Set the Shape pop-up to Square.

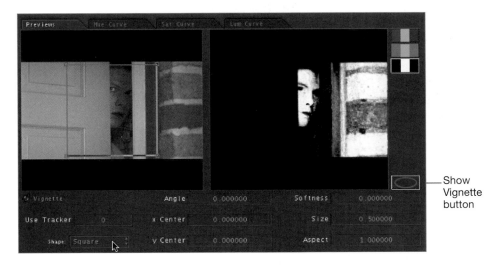

Show Vignette button

**3**   In the preview area, use the mask handles to position the mask around the entire open doorway area.

> **TIP** ▶ When the Matte Preview is set to desaturated preview, you can display the vignette shape in the Viewer using the Show Vignette button in the bottom right of the Previews tab.

While in desaturated preview mode, the Viewer shows the combined selection of the key and the vignette. Remember that the vignette always *adds* to the key selection. There is no way to subtract a vignette selection from a key selection.

**4**   Click the Final image button (red-green-blue).

The Viewer displays the shot in full color. Now you're ready to make your adjustment.

**5**  Drag the Midtone color balance control and watch the Vectorscope.

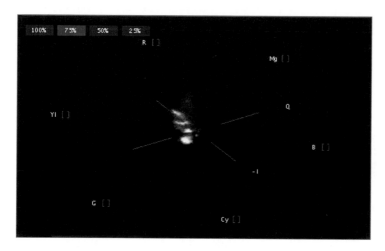

You can clearly identify the small blob of traces moving around that represent the skin tones of the face.

**6**  Click the 50% button in the Vectorscope to zoom in slightly on the traces in the scope.

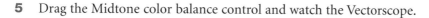

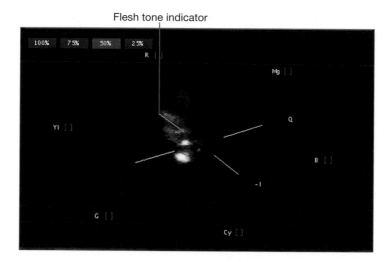

The upper-left bar of the diagonal yellow crosshairs in the Vectorscope indicates the color of natural-looking human flesh tones. Regardless of race or skin color, all human skin naturally fits very close to this particular color, and variations of skin darkness appear as a variety of saturation (the distance from the center of the scope).

As you drag your Midtone color balance control, you can easily move the color of the face so it sits right on that line, correcting the slightly red hue in the source footage.

**7** Drag the Midtone color balance control, watching the Vectorscope, until the traces representing the face sit squarely on the flesh tone line. Then drag away from the center (increasing saturation) until the traces just peek out from behind the other traces on the line.

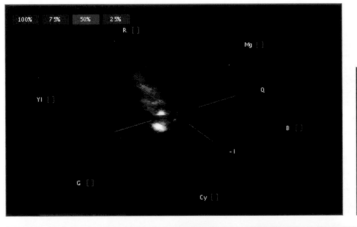

This corrects the slight red tint present in the source footage giving a healthy and natural look to the overall shot.

## Using Multiple Keys

Although correcting the skin tones of the actor's face improves the shot somewhat, now that you're in here making secondary corrections, you'll likely start looking around for other things to improve.

One thing that might come to mind is that the green door could do with some increased saturation. Although there are a number of ways to accomplish this, one option would be to do another key on the color of the door.

Because the key in secondary 1 is already working to isolate the face, you need to open a new secondary.

1  Click the "2" tab at the bottom of the Secondaries room.

This opens a brand new Secondaries room, ready for new settings. The secondary corrections in room #1 will still affect the clip. The results of the two Secondaries rooms will be combined in the final shot.

2  Click the eyedropper and drag the red crosshairs across the door in the Viewer to select the door's color.

**NOTE** ▶ Because you left the Preview mode set to Final in Secondaries room #1, room #2 will default to that same setting.

3  Click the Desaturated Preview mode button to check your selection in the Viewer.

**4**  Clean up the matte by Shift-dragging the right range handle of the Hue qualifier to the right to expand the color selection. If necessary, adjust the other qualifiers until the door is well selected.

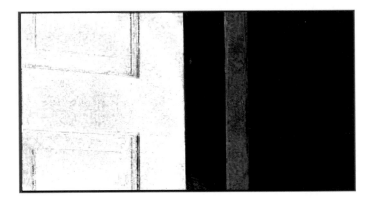

Don't worry too much about the doorjamb that's getting partially selected. It won't be affected very much by the saturation change you plan to make, and in the worst case, you could always add a vignette to eliminate it from your selection just like the brick in the previous exercise.

**5**  Middle-click the Key Blur control and drag to the right to set the blur to about 1.

Now the door is selected and ready for correcting.

**6**  Click the Final Image button (red-green-blue) to display the full image in the Viewer.

The goal is to add some saturation to the color, so you might be inclined to try boosting the Saturation slider in the Midtone color balance control.

**7**  Drag the Midtone Saturation slider.

Wait a minute! Rather than simply increasing the overall saturation, red is being added to the shot. This is not what you want.

**8**   Click the reset button for the Midtone color balance control.

**9**   Middle-click the Saturation parameter in the Basic tab beneath the keying controls and drag it to the right until it reaches about 1.5.

This control allows you to add saturation in a hue-neutral way. The other controls in this section work in a similar way.

**10**   Toggle Control-G to compare the graded image to the original.

This illustrates how you can combine multiple keys (and multiple secondaries in general) to create more complex effects. If you wanted to continue working on this image, you could do another secondary (using either a key or vignette) to isolate the bricks and finesse them as well.

Remember that your overall goal is to control the viewer's point of focus. If the door and the brick were very well highlighted using contrast or saturation, they would pull attention away from the actor (who is presumably the most important aspect of the shot). However, if you did the opposite—highlighting the actor's face—you could compensate for any possible confusion that the shot's inherent composition might create.

## Creating Custom Mask Shapes

By now, you've used vignettes in several examples but in each case you've used a very simple shape. The oval and rectangular masks accommodate an incredible range of situations; however, some shots require irregular and custom shapes. Color has a sophisticated tool for correcting such shots, using a combination of the Secondaries and Geometry rooms.

**1** Double-click the second shot in the Timeline (**Lakeside.move**) to make it active.

This shot already has some primary correction applied, but the man's jacket needs to be adjusted to make it match the other shots in the film. It can't be keyed because the color is too similar to some colors in the sky, the water, and possibly even some of the skin tones.

A simple oval or rectangular mask also won't work, due to the irregular shape of the jacket. The best solution is to employ a custom user-defined shape.

**2** Press Command-3 to bring the Secondaries room to the front (if it's not already there).

**3** Click the #1 tab at the bottom to make sure you're working on secondary #1.

> **NOTE ▶** Color will always default to showing the same secondary tab as used in the previous shot.

**4** Select the Enable checkbox, then select the Vignette checkbox.

**5** Set the Shape pop-up to User Shape.

The Geometry room is automatically opened, with the Shapes tab in front, and a new shape selected. The next click you make will begin to draw the shape.

**6** Click to add points that roughly outline the shape of the jacket. Don't worry about being too precise. Use the figure below as a guide.

7   When your shape matches the picture above, click the Close Shape button.

The shape is automatically closed. Color uses a system called *B-splines* to control the size and position of the shape. That means you manipulate points that construct a polygon surrounding the curved shape.

8   Adjust the points to make the shape more accurately surround the jacket.

TIP ▶ To move the entire mask as an object, drag the small green box with an X in it, in the center of the shape.

In Color, you can't delete points from your path, and you can only add points by opening the shape and adding more points to the end of the path.

**9**   Click Open Shape.

**10**  Add new points to make your shape exclude the black t-shirt.

**11**  Click Close Shape and make any necessary additional adjustments.

Most masks used for color correction benefit from edge softening to make the change in the affected area more subtle. While in the Secondaries room preview area you can soften a shape by middle-clicking and dragging the shape itself, in the Geometry room you must use the Softness slider.

**12**  Position your pointer over the Softness parameter name and roll the mouse scroll wheel upward to increase the softness of the shape to about .25.

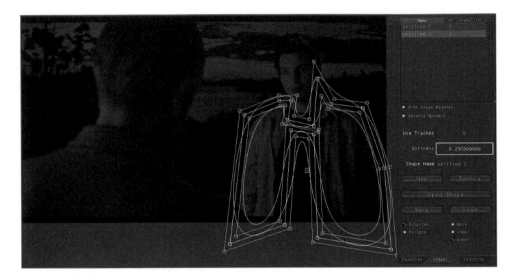

The softness is represented by two additional outlines, each with their own control points. This allows you to vary the amount of softness for different sections of the shape, as well as the inside versus the outside.

**13** Move the outside green handles so the actor's face and neck are totally outside the range of the shape.

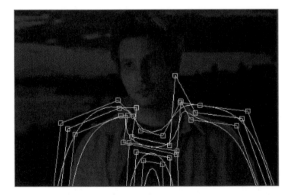

**14** Select the Hide Shape Handles checkbox to see the rough outline of the shape more clearly.

**15** When you're happy with your shape, click the Attach button at the top.

This assigns the shape to the currently active secondary vignette.

**16** Press Command-3 or click the Secondaries tab to bring the Secondaries room forward.

When the vignette is assigned to User Shape, all the vignette controls are dimmed, so any adjustments must be made in the Geometry room.

**17**  Click the Final Image button (red-green-blue).

**18**  Make sure the Control pop-up (in the upper right) is set to Inside.

**19**  Drag both the Midtone and Highlight color balance controls toward yellow to make the jacket appear more beige.

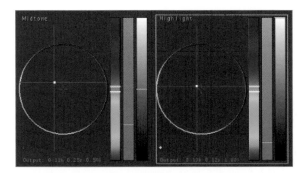

**20**  In the Timeline, press the spacebar to play the clip.

Now that you can see the effect in action, you may want to return to the Geometry room and further adjust the shape.

**21**  Find the frame where the man's arm is at its rightmost point.

**22**  Press Command-6 or click the Geometry tab to make that room active.

**23**  Click Hide Shape Handles to reactivate the handles.

**24** Manipulate the shape and the softness handles while watching the Viewer to make sure the highlight on the man's right side is included in the matte (or whatever other adjustments your mask may need).

By dragging the yellow points, you move the entire shape; by moving the green points, you manipulate the softness boundary.

> **TIP** ▶ If you ever have a shape where the position of the handles causes the shape to contain an unwanted loop, the Reverse Normals checkbox will swap the points' positions to eliminate the overlapping area. But beware: The change affects only the Final Preview in the Viewer; the lines in the Geometry room will not actually update.

It's common to go back and forth between the Secondaries and the Geometry rooms frequently as you finesse the custom-shaped vignette effect. If your shape ever gets totally screwed up, you can always click the Detach button and begin drawing an entirely new shape, then attach that one.

## Combining Vignettes

Vignettes are incredibly powerful, but often you need to combine several of them to adequately grade a shot. This is done using multiple Secondaries rooms, just like the earlier example involving multiple keys.

Although a number of vignettes can be applied to a single clip, Color does not allow you to subtract one mask shape from another (creating a doughnut hole) or otherwise combine multiple vignettes in complex ways, such as having two noncontiguous shapes treated as a single vignette. Each vignette allows you to change the settings within it, and if two masks overlap, applying the same settings to both would result in a double effect in the overlapping area.

In this exercise you'll add a lens vignette effect (a rounded edge darkening to the corners of the image) to the lakeside shot.

**1** Press Command-3 to bring the Secondaries room forward.

**2** Click the #2 tab to activate the second secondary.

The custom vignette on the jacket remains active, but a new Secondaries tab opens, ready for a new effect.

**3** Select the Enable and Vignette checkboxes.

**4** Set the Shape pop-up to Circle.

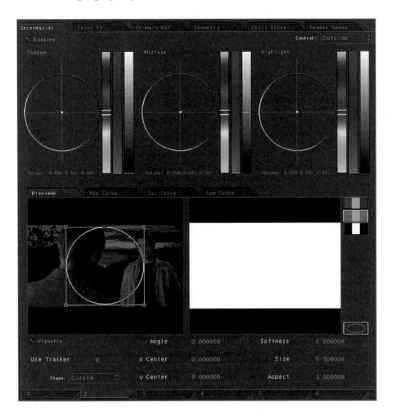

**5** In the Previews tab, adjust the shape until the circle just exceeds the frame.

**6**  Middle-click and drag on the shape to soften its edge.

**7**  Set the Control pop-up to Outside.

**8**  Drag the Shadow contrast slider down until a subtle darkening is visible in the corners of the frame in the Viewer.

**9**  Desaturate the outside by 15%. This will help to round off the edges.

**10**  Adjust the size, position, and softness of the shape as necessary.

**11**  Press Control-G to toggle the grade off and on to see the overall effect you've applied (including the Primary corrections that were done for you).

## Incorporating Curve Effects

Don't forget that each Secondary tab can also include curve-based effects to modify the hue, saturation, and luma of your shots based on hue.

The secondary curves do not observe the settings in the key or vignette sections of the room. Curve effects are limited only by the control points you set to determine the hue you want to modify. However, because the secondaries are applied in numerical order, applying the curves in different Secondaries rooms may result in different effects based on the other secondaries you apply, including other curve effects.

For example, if you change the color of the sky in this shot from orange to magenta in secondary #2 and then boost the saturation of magentas in secondary #3, the latter will affect the former.

> **NOTE** ▶ It's important to note that curve effects are not keyframable, so be careful when applying the effects to shots with dynamic contrast and color changes during a single take.

**1**　In secondary #2, click the Hue Curve tab.

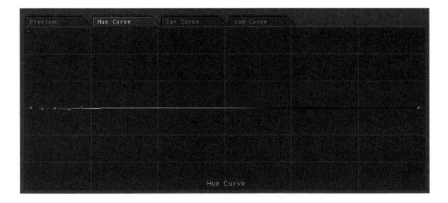

**2**　Add four points in the orange portion of the curve.

**3**　Raise the third point slightly to make the yellower tones more pink.

**4**　Lower the second point, making the redder tones more orange.

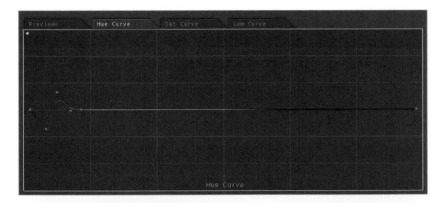

**5**   Click the #3 tab at the bottom of the Secondaries room.

**6**   Select the Enable checkbox to activate this secondary.

**7**   Click the Sat Curve tab.

**8**   Add points to boost the saturation of the orange colors and reduce the magenta.

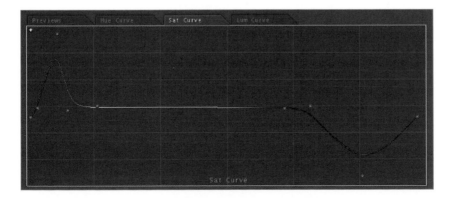

**TIP** ▶ In some cases you could apply a similar effect by just using two curves in the same secondary. However, breaking them into separate secondaries this way allows you to turn them on and off independently using the Enable checkbox for each secondary room.

The curve in secondary #3 affects the results of the secondaries that came before it. If you were to go back to secondary #1 and change the man's jacket to a pink or orange color, it, too, would be affected by the results of these curve adjustments.

Understanding how the different secondaries affect one another allows you to combine your effects in complex and interesting ways. For example, if you had made the man's jacket pink and wanted to boost the pink sky, but not the pink jacket, you would need to apply the jacket correction to a higher-numbered secondary.

Similarly, if you wanted a curve effect to be altered by a mask or key effect, you would need to apply it to a lower-numbered secondary.

Obviously these exercises only scratch the surface of what can be done by combining multiple secondaries in a single shot. Although applying many secondaries can increase render times, there is no reason not to employ them liberally to create fantastic and unique looks for all of your shots.

## Lesson Review

1. True or false: Keys and vignettes can be combined in a single secondary operation.
2. How many secondaries can be applied to a single clip?
3. How do you control only one side of the HSL qualifiers?
4. What control indicates proper flesh tone values?

5. How can you apply two key effects to a single clip?

6. Where can you adjust saturation in a color-neutral way?

7. How many points can a custom shape contain?

8. Can you add and delete points from a custom shape? If so, how and where?

9. Where can you control the softness of the inside of a shape independently from the outside softness?

10. How do you create a doughnut-hole effect where one mask punches out another?

11. Are secondaries applied in ascending or descending order?

12. Are the Hue, Sat, and Lum curves limited by key or vignette settings?

*Answers*

1. True.

2. There are eight Secondaries rooms for each clip, but multiple effects can be created in a single room.

3. Shift-drag the handle you desire to move independently.

4. The upper-left diagonal line in the Vectorscope.

5. Use two secondary operations.

6. The Saturation controls in the Basic tab affect all colors uniformly.

7. There is no limit to the number of control points on a custom shape.

8. In the Geometry room, points can be added by opening the end, but cannot be added between two existing points. Points cannot be deleted.

9. The Geometry room preview allows you to drag the softness points independently. This requires first increasing the mask softness control.

10. Masks cannot be combined in this manner.

11. Ascending.

12. No. Curves ignore keys and vignettes.

# 5

**Lesson Files**  Color Book Files > Lesson Files > Lesson 05 > GradeMgmt.colorproj

**Time**  This lesson takes approximately 120 minutes to complete.

**Goals**  Utilize multiple grades on individual clips

Switch between saved grades to compare looks

Add and delete grades from shots and groups

Save and restore both individual corrections and grades

Move grades from one clip to another in different ways

Create and manage groups of clips to consolidate work

Move grades to and from groups and individual clips

# Lesson 5
# Grade Management

Effective grading is a subtle and subjective art. The fickle client who requests endless changes (often ending up right where you started) is so common, he's almost a cliché. A good colorist knows this and plans ahead, storing different versions of each shot's corrections so she can easily compare looks, make changes procedurally, and when needed, quickly revert to an earlier grade.

Additionally, most shows repeat shots within each scene. The most common example of this is a typical dialogue scene where the editor cuts back and forth frequently between similar camera setups and angles. These repeated shots will most likely require the exact same color adjustments, so once you've graded one, you can simply reapply that same grade to the other similar shots.

And finally, long-form documentary and drama programs frequently repeat locations, which may or may not have been shot on the same day under similar lighting conditions. It's a critical part of the colorist's job to make these scenes appear consistent. Although this might seem a straightforward task, you can quickly work yourself into a frenzy by tweaking shot two to match shot one, then going back and adjusting shot one to match shot two, and so on.

Color is designed to assist colorists who find themselves in all of these situations. It provides a variety of ways to streamline and simplify what could otherwise be cumbersome and complicated project management tasks. This lesson will familiarize you with many of the most common grade management tasks.

## Managing Grades on a Single Shot

No matter what type of shot you're correcting, you'll likely want to experiment with some alternative grades before committing to a final choice. In Color, each shot can have four grades stored at any one time, and you can switch between them with a simple keystroke.

**1** Open Lessons Files > Lesson 05 > **GradeMgmt.colorproj.**

This project contains a full scene from a sample movie. The first few shots have already been graded.

**2** Choose File > Reconnect Media and navigate to Lesson Files > Lesson 05 > Media, then click Choose.

**3** Right-click (or Control-click) the Timeline ruler and drag to zoom in on the first few clips.

The grades track beneath the clips displays the different grades applied to each clip. The first clip has three different grades applied, and grade 2 is active. Grade 2 contains a Primary In (PI) and three secondaries. Each of these corrections appears as a colored bar in the grade track area beneath the three grades.

**4** Press Command-2 to make the Primary In room active.

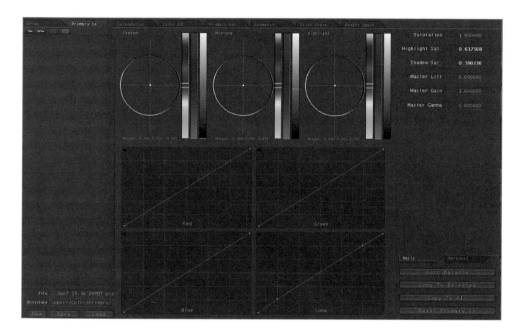

It might not be obvious from looking at the viewer what settings have been adjusted, but in the Primary In room you can see that the Luma curve has some points added, and the Highlight Sat. and Shadow Sat. controls in the Basic tab have numerical values in yellow (indicating that they're not at their default setting).

**5**    Press Command-3 to open the Secondaries room.

From the green bars in the Timeline grade track, you can see which Secondaries rooms are in use (1, 2, and 8).

**6** Click Secondaries tab 1 (if it isn't already active).

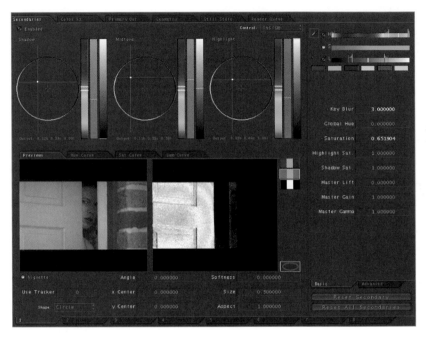

**7** Click the Final Image button (red-green-blue) to display the results of the secondary correction in the viewer.

**8** Select the Enable checkbox, and then deselect it again.

This allows you to see exactly how Secondary 1 is affecting the image. In this case, a key is applied to select the door and the color balance controls are adjusted to shade the door a yellow color.

**9**   Click Secondaries tab 2.

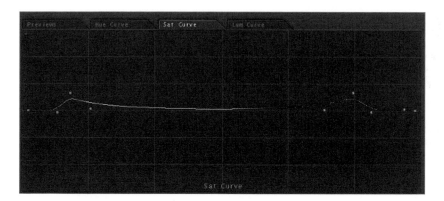

This secondary is employing a Sat curve to boost the saturation of the character's face.

**10**   Toggle the Enable checkbox and watch the Vectorscope to see this secondary's impact.

**11**   Click Secondaries tab 8.

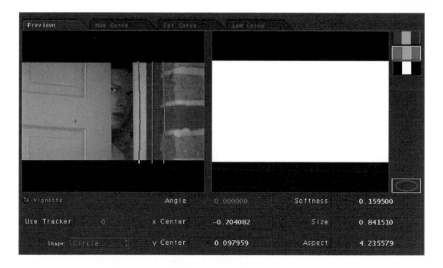

This secondary has the Vignette checkbox selected, and a simple rectangle shape is being used to limit the effect on the bricks.

If you don't see any settings that seem to be active, be sure to check both the Inside and the Outside control areas.

**12** Set the Control pop-up to Outside.

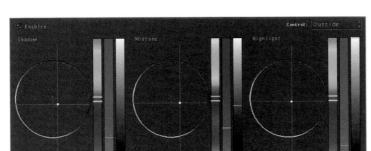

The color balance controls update to display the settings that are affecting the bricks.

**13** Press Control-G to turn the whole grade on and off.

Overall, this is a very heavy grade, using a variety of controls to manipulate the image in numerous ways.

## Switching Between Grades

When you have a shot with more than one grade applied to it, you can quickly switch between the grades to compare their effects. This is an essential and powerful tool that enables you to effectively evaluate a variety of grading options before settling on your final choice.

Color has four grade settings for each clip.

**1** Choose Grade > Grade 1 or press Control-1 to switch to grade 1.

Grade 1 has a very different look. Observing the grade track also indicates that it contains one primary and two secondaries. The grade track changes contents depending on what kind of corrections are used in the currently active grade.

You can also change grades directly in the grade track.

**2**   Click grade 3 in the grade track to switch to that grade.

This grade has only the primary and one secondary grade applied to it.

**3**   Press Control-1, Control-2, and Control-3 to switch between the different looks.

Switching between grades does not affect the settings within those grades. Any changes you make in the various rooms will automatically be saved as part of the currently active grade. For this reason, when working with multiple grades, it's important to keep track of which grade is currently active.

**4**   Drag the grade track divider (the gray line beneath the grade track in the Timeline) upward until the track is at its minimum height.

When the grade track is collapsed in this way, you won't be able to see which grade is currently active.

5    Drag the grade track divider back down to expand the track and reveal all the grades and corrections.

**NOTE** ▶ In some situations, Color will not update the contents of the grade track as you add or remove corrections. To force the grade track display to update, switch back and forth to another grade.

## Adding and Deleting Grades

When you begin working on a clip in Color, any corrections you make are saved in grade 1. If you want to leave the grade 1 settings alone and make changes to another grade instead, you must first add that additional grade.

This first clip already has three grades applied, so there's only one more possible grade to add.

1    Choose Grade > Grade 4 or press Control-4.

A fourth grade bar appears in the grade track and is made active.

2    Press Command-2 to open the Primary In room and make some adjustments to the clip.

3    Press Control-2 to switch to grade 2.

The clip reverts to the setting saved in grade 2. The changes you just made haven't been lost, however; they've been saved in grade 4.

4    Press Control-4 to switch back to grade 4.

Your custom settings are restored.

5   Right-click grade 4 in the grade track and choose Remove Grade 4 from the short-cut menu.

The grade is removed, and grade 1 is automatically set as active.

**TIP** ▶ Rather than deleting the grade, you could also have chosen Reset Grade 4, which would clear any corrections you may have applied, while leaving the grade intact in the grade track.

**NOTE** ▶ If there is only one grade applied to a clip, it cannot be removed.

## Duplicating a Grade

One of the most common workflows employing multiple grades is to create a grade, then make an alternative version that is mostly the same but with some modifications. For example, in this first shot of the man answering the door, you might set the overall contrast to your liking, but then want to experiment with different colors for the door.

Once you get grade 1 set, you don't want to have to recreate it in grade 2; you simply want to duplicate it into grade 2, then make modifications to that duplicate. Although Color doesn't have a specific command for this common task, you can accomplish it very easily employing a special type of copy and paste.

In addition to the four grades assignable to each clip, Color has five "memory banks" specifically for grades. By copying your grade into one of those banks, you can paste it into another grade on the same clip, creating the duplicate you desire.

**TIP** ▶ You can also paste it onto another clip, but we'll get to that later in this lesson.

1   Press Control-2 to make grade 2 the active grade.

2   Choose Grade > Copy Grade > Mem-bank 1 or press Control-Shift-Option-1.

All aspects of the grade are saved into the memory bank. This memory bank will store your grade until you copy a new grade into that slot, or until you quit Color.

3   Press Control-4 to create grade 4.

**4** Choose Grade > Paste Grade > Mem-bank 1 or press Shift-Option-1.

Grade 2 is "duplicated" into grade 4. Now you can make changes to that grade, and at any point switch back to grade 2 to revisit your original settings.

## Setting the Beauty Grade

In this example the looks you're choosing between are dramatically different from one another. But in the real world, often your different grades may have only subtle differences, and it's fairly easy to lose track of your preference.

Color has a way to keep track of your current "favorite," regardless of which grade is currently active. It's called the *beauty grade*.

**1** Press Control-3 to activate grade 3.

**2** Choose Grade > Set Beauty Grade or press Shift-Control-B.

Grade 3 turns Orange in the grade track.

**NOTE** ► The beauty grade is nothing more than a marker. It has no impact on the image whatsoever, and does not affect which grade is currently active.

**3** Press Control-2 to switch back to grade 2.

The active grade appears blue, and the beauty grade remains orange. When the beauty grade is active, it stays orange. There can be only one beauty grade per clip.

**NOTE ▶** Once a beauty grade has been applied to a clip, you can change which grade it is set to, but you cannot remove it without deleting the current beauty grade altogether.

## Saving Corrections and Grades

All the work you do grading shots is valuable time spent, and most shows will require very similar corrections across many different clips. Furthermore, some settings can even be used across multiple projects. For these reasons, Color allows you to save both individual corrections and whole grades to files on your hard disk, so you can reuse them in other projects, bring them with you when moving to a new workstation, or even share them with other colorists.

These saved settings are easily accessible from within Color and can be quickly applied to other shots in a variety of ways.

### ▶ Corrections Versus Grades

At the end of Lesson 1 you learned about the terms color *correcting* and color *grading* and how the terms are frequently used interchangeably. In Color, the noun forms of these terms (corrections and grades) have specific meaning, with an important distinction.

Settings made in an individual room (Primary In, Secondary 3, etc.) are called *corrections*, whereas the combination of corrections created across multiple rooms on a single clip is called a *grade*.

Both corrections and grades can be saved as files, and in fact, if you peek inside a saved grade (which is actually a folder), you'll find multiple correction files that correspond to the rooms that had active settings when the grade was originally saved.

**1** Double-click the second clip in the Timeline (**MLS_Henry_02**).

This clip has one grade applied, containing a Primary In correction and two secondaries.

**2** Press Command-2 to open the Primary In room.

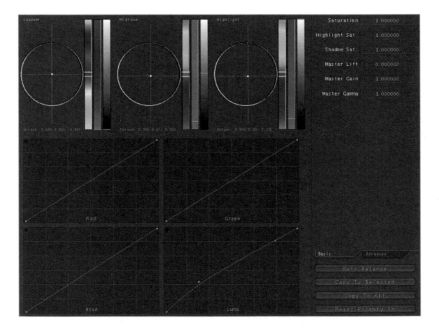

A variety of settings have been adjusted, and for the purpose of the lesson, assume the correction is exactly the way you want it.

Up until this point, we have basically ignored the file list area on the left side of the Primary In room. This area is specifically for storing Primary In corrections.

Parent Directory
Home Directory        Icon Size Slider

Icon View        List View

**3**    In the File field in the lower-left corner of the Primary In room, type
*MSHenryCorrection_01*.

**4**    Leave the Directory setting to the default value (which is Home > Library >
Application Support > Color > Primary).

**5**    Click the Save button.

The correction is saved as a file, and an item appears in the file list area, representing
the saved correction.

**6**    If your file view area isn't displaying icons, click the Icon View button.

**NOTE ▶** You can choose to save your corrections to any directory you like, but
by selecting another location, you will need to navigate there manually to recall the
saved correction.

**7**    Use the slider at the top of the file list area to adjust the size of the thumbnail.

**8** Click the List View button to change the view to a list.

Reapplying a saved correction is simple and straightforward. As you might expect, you can apply it to other clips (which you'll do in the next exercise) or you can reapply it to a different grade on the same clip.

**9** Press Control-2 to add a second grade to the clip.

**10** Double-click the saved grade in the file list.

Those settings are applied to the Primary In room of grade 2.

Now you can make adjustments to that grade, and easily return to the saved state if you change your mind.

**NOTE ▶** You may need to click grade 1 in the grade track and then return to grade 2 to confirm that your grade is applied.

**11** Adjust the Blue curve to cool the overall balance of the shot.

This modification changes the look of the shot. If you're happy with this as an alternative grade, you can keep it (keep in mind that you already have the old Primary In settings stored in grade 1). However, if you don't like the changes, you can easily revert to the saved state.

**12** Double-click the saved correction in the file list (or select it and click the Load button).

The room is restored to the saved state.

> **TIP** Color doesn't have a multiple undo feature, so saving your corrections frequently as you work allows you to step backwards through your work, almost like a manual "history palette."

**13** Switch the file list back to Icon view.

## Deleting Saved Corrections

The file list area simply looks for certain file types on your hard disk. Because these are saved files, they'll be available to different projects and can even be moved around. The downside to this is that you can quickly build up quite a few saved corrections cluttering your file list.

Deleting saved corrections can be done directly in the file list in Color, or manually in the Finder. In order to demonstrate deleting them, it will be helpful to create a few new saved corrections.

**1** Make any change to the Primary In controls and click the Save button.

**2** Repeat step 1.

Two new corrections are added to the file list.

**NOTE** ▶ If you don't add a custom name prior to saving, the date and time are used as the filename. These names are not editable in Color once the file has been saved.

3   Select one of the new grades in the file list and press Delete (or Forward-Delete).

Color warns you that deleting saved corrections is not undoable.

4   Click Yes.

The correction is deleted forever.

## Organizing Corrections

Another approach to managing your saved corrections is to organize them into subfolders. Color allows you to create new folders directly in the file list. However, you must plan ahead: Corrections can't be moved from one folder to another (inside Color) once they've been created.

1   Click the New Folder button (at the bottom of the file list area).

**NOTE** ▶ On lower-resolution monitors, this button name may be truncated to "New."

A dialog appears asking you to name the new folder.

2   Type *Henry Primaries* and click Create.

A new folder is added, and the file list displays the contents of that new folder (which is empty).

**3**  Type a name in the File field and click Save.

Your correction is saved in the new folder.

**4**  Click the Parent Directory button (the leftmost button at the top of the file list).

The file list displays the directory containing the folder you created in step 1.

Although organizing your corrections into folders and subfolders (typically named for each project, and then each shot, respectively) is smart, in practice, it's hard to anticipate your corrections well enough to get everything in the right folders, especially because Color won't allow you to rename or rearrange the corrections once they've all been created.

Fortunately, because they're all just files and folders on your hard disk, you can easily clean them up in the Finder.

**5**    Switch to the Finder.

**6**    Navigate to Home > Library > Application Support > Color > Primary.

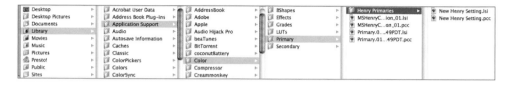

Here you can freely rename and rearrange your corrections, adding folders and sub-folders however you wish. Each correction is saved as a pair of files. The .lsi file is the thumbnail and the .pcc file is the correction settings. You should always move them together.

**7**    Create a new folder, name it *Alternate Henry Looks*, and drag some of the correction files into it.

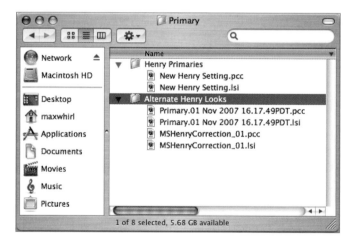

**8**    Switch back to Color.

**9**    In the file list, click the Home button (the second button from the top-left).

> **NOTE ▸** If the Home button returns you to a different folder, you can click the Parent directory button to navigate to the Color > Primary folder.

The file list is refreshed to display the folder you just created in the Finder.

## Saving Secondary Corrections

All of the techniques you used in saving Primary corrections can be applied in the Secondaries room as well. The only difference is that you must remember that saving a secondary correction actually saves the exact state of *all eight* secondary rooms. Even if some of the rooms are disabled or unused, all of their settings will be saved—and replaced—if you apply a saved secondary to a clip.

1   In the Timeline, press the Down Arrow to move the selection to the third clip (**CU_Midge_03**).

    This clip has two secondaries applied, rooms 1 and 8.

2   Press Command-3 to switch to the Secondaries room, and click through the tabs to see the effects applied.

3   Triple-click the default name in the File field to select all of it and then type *Midge_Look1* and click Save to save this Secondary.

The secondary corrections are saved as a file.

**4**    Click the Secondary 2 tab to make that room active.

**5**    Select the Enable checkbox and click the preview tab if it's not already selected.

**6**    Select the Vignette checkbox, set the shape to Circle, and mask the area of the striped wall on the left side of the frame (use the figure below as a guide).

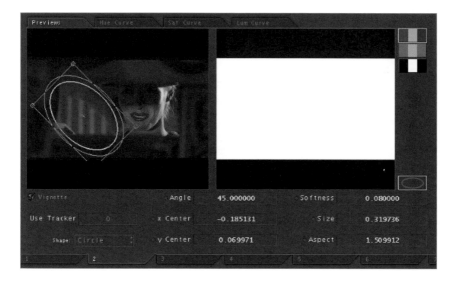

**7**    Make sure Control is set to Inside and lower the Highlight contrast slider until the stripes (visible as the staggered white dots) are lowered to about 40% in the Waveform Monitor.

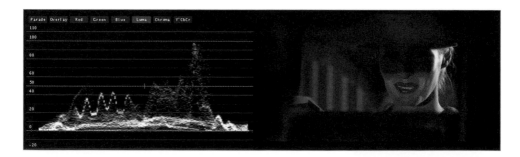

This helps direct the viewer's point of focus toward the woman's face.

**8**    Type *DimStripes* in the File field and click Save.

The correction is saved in the file list.

**9**    Click the Reset All Secondaries button in the lower-right corner of the room.

All secondaries are reset and disabled.

**10**    Double-click the Midge Look 1 correction.

Secondaries 1 and 8 are turned on, and restored to the saved settings.

**11**    Double-click the DimStripes correction.

That saved state is applied to the shot.

## Saving Grades

So far you've saved and reapplied corrections in the Primary In and Secondaries rooms individually. Color also has a way to save all of the corrections across all the rooms into a single grade. Because these saved grades are not tied to one particular type of correction, they are managed in the Setup room.

**1**    Press Command-1 to open the Setup room.

**2**    Click the Grades tab. The grades tab contains a file list nearly identical to the file lists in the Primary In and Secondaries rooms. The only difference is that this one stores whole grades rather than individual corrections.

**3**    Double-click the first clip in the sequence to select it.

**4**    Click the New Folder button in the Grades tab of the Setup room.

**5**    Name the folder Lesson 05 and click the Create button.

**6**    Type *Shot 1 Custom Grade* in the File field and click the Save button.

The grade is saved.

**NOTE** ▶ Applying a saved grade to a new clip will obliterate any existing corrections on that clip in any room.

### Removing Grades in the Finder

Saved grades actually contain saved corrections within them. If for any reason you want to extract one of the individual corrections, you can do so in one of two ways. First of all, once the grade is applied to a clip, you can always go to the room for the corrections you want to save (Primary In, Secondaries, Color FX, and so on) and save the correction there using the steps from the previous lesson.

Alternatively, you can remove the grades in the Finder.

**1**  Switch to the Finder.

**2**  Navigate to Home > Library > Application Support > Color > Grades > Lesson 5.

**3**  Right-click the Shot 1 Custom Grade.colorgrade file and choose Show Package Contents.

The "file" opens as if it were a folder, and the individual grades are contained inside. You could manually copy one of these grades into another folder (along with a copy of the .lsi thumbnail file) and navigate to that folder from within the Primary In or another room's file list. If you do this, be sure to include a copy of the .lsi file with each of the other grades you extract. Otherwise, there will be no thumbnail visible in the Color file lists.

**TIP** ▶ Your Color projects are also packages that can be opened in the Finder to expose all of the corrections, thumbnails, and other elements used in your project. Although this procedure is not always for the faint of heart, it's good to know all those elements are accessible if you need them.

## Moving Grades from Clip to Clip

All of this grade and correction management is useful for single clips, but it becomes downright essential when dealing with shows that repeat similar clips across scenes and sequences—and what show doesn't?

Like most aspects of Color, there are many ways to accomplish this common task, and you'll likely apply different ones in different situations. First of all, you can use the grade memory banks to copy and paste grades from one shot to another, just like you did to move corrections between grades on the same shot earlier.

Also, by saving corrections or grades into files as you did in the previous exercises, you can easily apply those saved settings to new clips.

1    In Color, make sure the Setup room is open and the Grades tab is displayed.

2    In the Timeline, press the Down Arrow until you reach the next instance of the doorway clip (clip 10).

3    In the Grades tab, drag the grade you saved in the previous exercise to the clip's grade track in the Timeline.

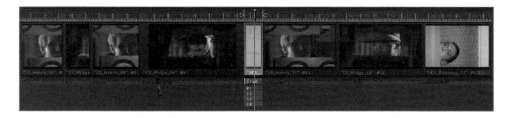

The settings stored in the saved grade are applied to the selected clip. If there were previously any corrections applied to the clip (in the current grade) they will be replaced.

### Applying Saved Settings to a New Grade

Alternatively, you can choose to apply the settings to a new grade (rather than replacing the contents of the existing grade). You might do this if you want to see how the grade looks on a different clip, without necessarily removing the existing grade you've already created.

1   Press Home to navigate to the beginning of the Timeline and double-click the third clip (**CU_Midge_03**).

This clip already has a grade applied, but perhaps you want to see how the grade from the doorway shot looks on it.

2   Press Control-2 to activate grade 2 on this shot.

3   Drag the saved grade from the Grades tab to the clip.

**TIP** If you drag to the main clip in the Timeline, the settings will be applied to the currently active grade. Alternatively, you can drag directly to one of the grade bars in the grade track to apply it to a different grade.

The settings are applied to grade 2.

**NOTE** ▶ Remember that sometimes Color's grade track won't automatically update to show the change. Switching to another shot and/or another grade will usually force the Timeline display to update.

Applying individual corrections from one clip to another can also be accomplished by following this same procedure. The only difference is that you drag the saved correction from the file list in the Primary In or Secondaries room instead of from the Grades tab. Corrections will be applied to the corresponding room of the current grade, replacing any existing settings in that room.

### Using the Copy To Buttons

The Primary In and Out rooms have a built-in way to copy their settings to other clips—either to selected clips or to every clip in your project. There are two buttons in the lower-right corner of the room (below the Auto Balance button).

This makes sense as many scenes are shot in a single location under similar circumstances and the basic "balancing" you apply will likely be the same or very similar for all of those shots.

1   Double-click the fourth shot (**CU_Henry_04**) to make it active.

2   Press Command-2 to open the Primary In room.

    The primary corrections applied to this clip are already done, so you're ready to copy them to other similar clips in your show. But can you apply these settings to every clip? Or should you only copy them to some of the clips?

3   Press Shift-Command-M to toggle your Timeline playback to Movie mode.

4   Press the spacebar to play the sequence.

    Although many of the clips are from the same location and in similar lighting conditions, some of them are clearly different. There is no way you'd want to use the same settings on the outside doorway shot as the inside pizza box shots. This rules out using the Copy To All button. But clearly you might choose to copy these settings to some of the other clips.

5   Double-click again on the fourth clip to make it active.

**6**   Press Shift-Command-M to return to clip-based playback.

**7**   Click once to select the sixth clip (another copy of the same shot).

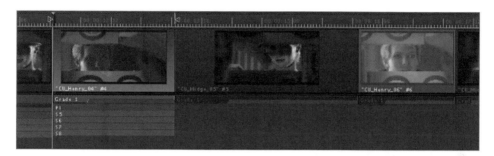

The blue highlight indicates that the clip is selected, and the gray highlight on the fourth clip indicates that it's the active clip. (Its settings are the ones displayed in the Primary In room above.)

**8**   In the Primary In room, click the Copy To Selected button.

**9**   Double-click the sixth clip to verify that the primary settings have been applied there.

## Dragging and Dropping Grades

Another way to move corrections from one clip to another is to drag them right in the grade track of the Timeline. You can drag whole grades or individual corrections.

**1**   Move and/or Zoom the Timeline so you can clearly see shots 3 through 10 in the Timeline. (It's easy to spot clip 10, because you applied corrections to it earlier and none of the surrounding clips have any corrections applied.)

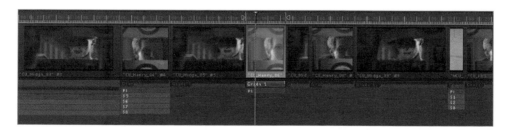

You can see by looking at the thumbnails in the Timeline that there are several instances of both the CU_Henry and the CU_Midge shots. In the last exercise, you copied just the primary correction from shot 4 to shot 6, but in this case you want the whole grade (containing both primary and secondary corrections).

2   Drag the grade 1 from shot 4 onto grade 1 of shot 6.

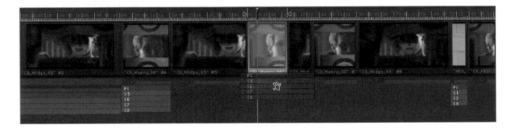

The grade is copied from one clip to the other. You can also use this technique to copy the contents of one grade to another grade on the same clip.

**TIP** ▶ To preserve any existing settings in grade 1 on shot 6, you could have enabled grade 2 on shot 6, then dragged grade 1 from shot 4 onto that new grade.

## Dragging Individual Corrections

You can drag individual corrections from one clip to another or one grade to another. Primary corrections will replace any Primary settings in the destination grade. Secondaries will replace only settings in the same Secondaries room. If no such secondary exists, it will be added.

It's unlikely that you'd move a secondary from one shot to another containing different footage (secondaries are too specifically tied to the contents of the scene). But when dragging between two instances of the same shot, or from one grade to another on the same shot, it can be a great time-saver.

1   Double-click the fourth shot (the first instance of CU_Henry) to make it active.

This shot currently has one grade, containing a primary and four secondaries. You might be happy with some aspects of the grade but not others. Rather than changing the grade itself, you can create a new one containing some, but not all, of the grade 1 corrections.

**2**   Press Control-2 to add a second grade to the shot.

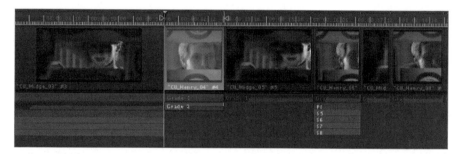

This makes grade 2 active, but to move corrections out of grade 1, grade 1 must be selected.

**3**   Click grade 1 in the grade track to make it active.

**4**   Drag S5 from grade 1 to grade 2.

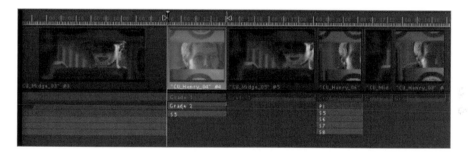

Grade 2 now contains only that secondary.

Although all this dragging and dropping is quick and easy and has its place in your workflow, it's not without peril. Rather than doing your work by looking at the Viewer and making unique adjustments in the rooms on each shot, you're hoping that part-and-parcel moving from one place to another will do the job. In some cases it very well might, but don't forget to watch every shot and make sure the grade works.

## Grouping Shots

Of course, in many shows you can safely copy grades from one shot to another because the shots are from the exact same footage. To accommodate this common situation, Color has a shot-grouping feature that allows you to apply a grade to every instance of a shot in one step.

To begin grouping, you must first identify all the shots you want to group. Rather than doing that in the Timeline, it's often easier to use the Shots browser in the Setup room.

**1**   Press Command-1 to open the Setup room.

**2**   Click the Shots tab to open the Shots browser.

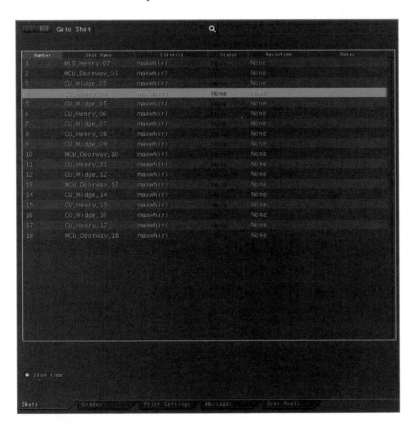

Just like the file viewer and grades, the Shots browser can be displayed in either icon or list view.

**3**   If it's not already displayed, click the List View button.

The clips are displayed in a list. You can sort the list by any of the columns by clicking on the header area.

**4**   Click the Shot Name header to sort the clips by that column.

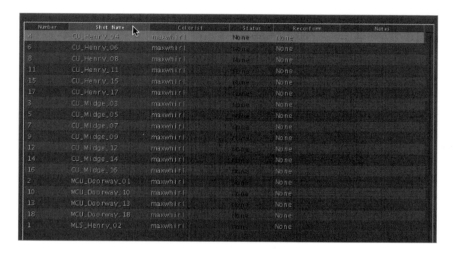

Now it's easy to see which shots are from the same source media.

**5**   Shift-select all of the CU_Henry shots.

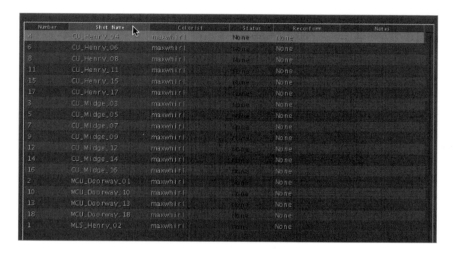

With all the clips selected you're ready to define those clips as a group. However, grouping can be done only in icon view.

6    Click the Icon View button.

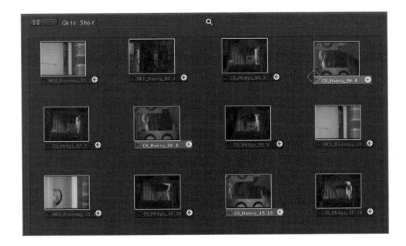

The clips remain selected, as indicated by the cyan highlight on the clip names. The cyan diamond indicates the currently active clip.

7    Right-click and drag any blank space in the window to zoom in and out. Zoom the view out until you can see all the clips.

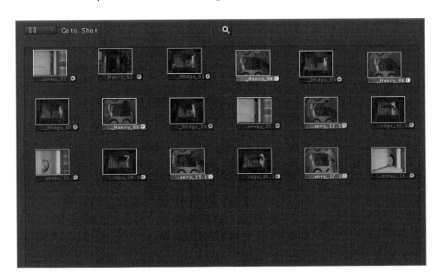

The Henry clips remain selected.

8   Press Command-G to group the clips.

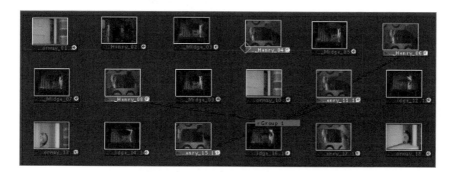

A new object is added to the icon view: a bar without an icon that represents the group. All of the grouped clips are tethered to the group by blue lines.

9   Drag the group icon to separate it visually from the other clips.

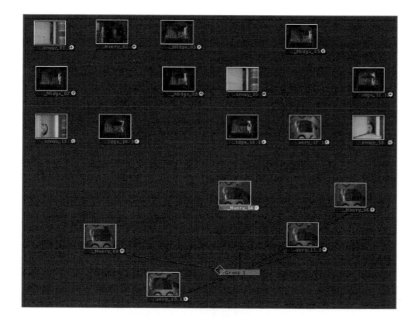

The remaining shots can also be grouped.

**10** Zoom out give yourself some more workspace, then drag the four shots of the doorway into a row, away from the other clips.

   **NOTE** ▶ You can drag clips only by their names, not by the icons themselves.

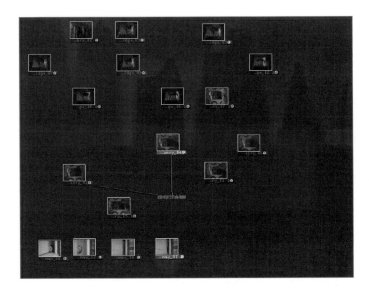

**11** Shift-click to select all four clips and press Command-G to create a second group.

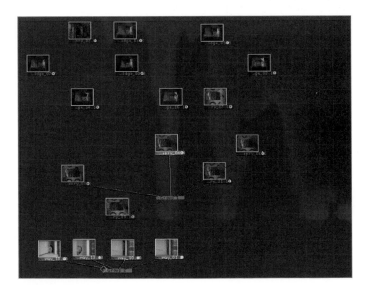

Almost all of the remaining clips are of Midge, and so can be grouped together. However, Shift-clicking all the remaining icons can be tedious. It's much quicker to select the clips in list view.

**12** Click the List View button.

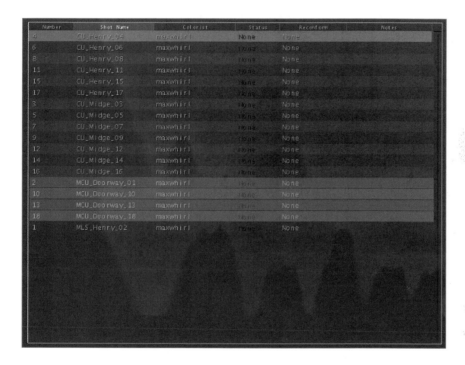

The clips should remain sorted the same way they were last time you used this view, and the four doorway clips are selected because they were selected in the icon view.

**13** Select the seven CU_Midge clips.

**14** Switch back to icon view and press Command-G to make a group of the Midge clips.

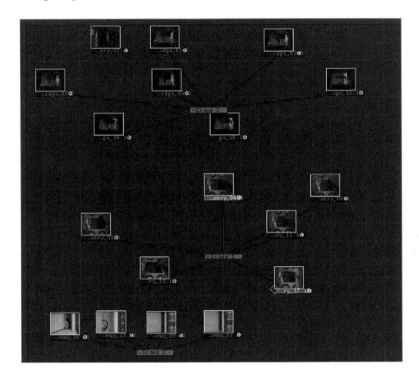

The only clip not included in any group is the MS_Henry shot. There's no reason every clip must be included in a group, but because this is another shot of Henry, in the same setting, perhaps it might benefit from sharing the same grade settings as the rest of the Henry shots. You can add and remove clips from a group directly in the icon view.

**15** Drag the MS_Henry shot until it's near the other Henry shots.

**16** Right-click the name and drag to add a blue line to the clip. Drag the blue line to connect it with the CU_Henry group icon.

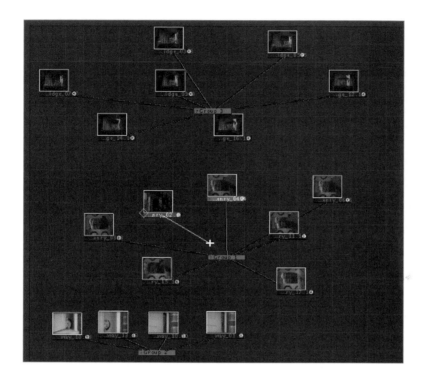

If at any point you change your mind about a grouping, and want to remove a clip from the group, that's easily done as well.

**17** Right-click and drag from the name of MS_Henry to any blank place in the window.

The clip is removed from the group.

If you like, you can clean up your icon view by moving the clips and the groups around to prevent confusing overlapping objects or grouping lines.

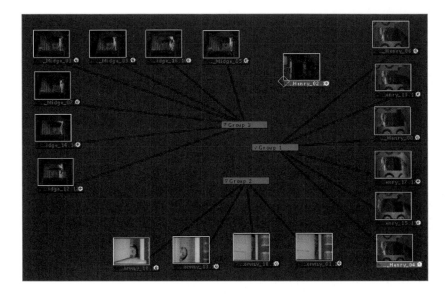

Putting clips into groups doesn't have any impact on their grades. If the shots previously had grades applied to them, adding or removing them from a group won't affect those existing grades. Grouping merely provides a way for you to apply a grade to multiple clips simultaneously.

Furthermore, once you've applied a grade to a group, any adjustments you make on any single clip will have no effect on the other clips in its group. This is good in that it allows you to use the group to apply a base grade, then tweak each clip individually to optimize its look.

## Applying Grades to Groups

Now that you've successfully grouped your clips, it's time to apply some grades to those clips. Grades can be applied to groups only by dragging a grade that has already been applied to a clip from the Timeline to the group icon in the icon view of the Shots browser.

That means that before you can apply a grade to a group, you must first create or apply that grade to a clip (probably one in the group). For this lesson, all the grades have already been created, and have been applied to at least one of the clips for each group.

**1**    In the Timeline, drag the grade 1 bar from the first CU_Midge shot to the group icon in the Shots browser. CU_Midge doesn't need to be selected or active.

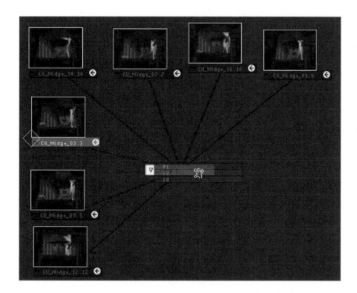

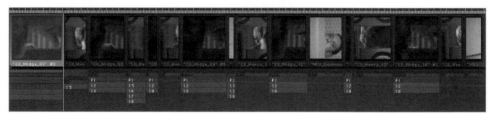

The grade is instantly applied to all the clips in the group. Any grade 1 settings on any clip within the group (in any room) will be replaced with the settings from the grade you just dragged.

If you want to change the grade for that shot, you must repeat this process.

**2**    Double-click any of the CU_Midge clips.

> **TIP** ▶  Because all the clips now have the exact same grade settings, it doesn't matter which one you activate.

3    Press Command-2 to open the Primary In room.

4    Drag the Midtone color balance control toward red-orange to add a little more warmth to the shot.

   This one shot is updated, but none of the others in the group have been affected. If your intention was to make the correction on this one shot, you're done. If, however, you want to update this change across all the shots in the group, you must do one more step.

5    Press Command-1 to return to the Setup room. The Shots browser should still be open and in icon view.

6    Drag the grade 1 bar from the active clip in the Timeline to the group icon for CU_Midge in the Shots browser.

   The new grade is reapplied to each of the other clips of the group.

## Working with Multiple Grades

If you include clips containing more than one grade in a group, or if you want to apply more than one grade to a group, you must ensure the source and destination grade numbers are consistent.

For example, if you drag grade 2 from the first doorway shot onto the doorway group, and the other instances of the doorway shot only have 1 active grade, the grade 2 settings will be applied to the grade 1 setting on those other clips. This may or may not be your intention.

1    Drag the grade 2 bar from the first clip in the Timeline to the group icon for the doorway shots in the Shots browser.

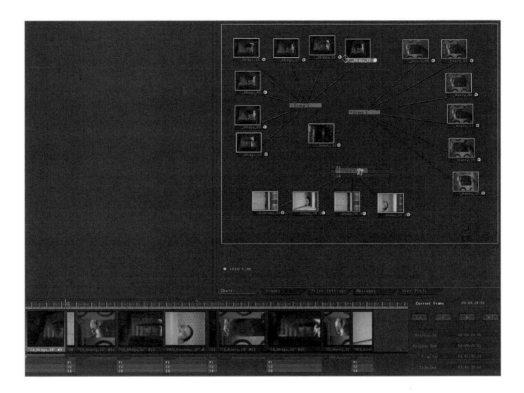

Not only have you just replaced any grade 1 settings on the other three instances of that shot, but on the first shot, the grade was reapplied to grade 2, leaving grade 1 alone.

**2**   To apply multiple grades to a group, manually apply additional (empty) grades to each item in the group, then drag grades to each of those slots.

### Resetting Grades
If you ever go so far down the wrong path that you simply want to reset your entire grade to default settings, there is a quick and easy way to do it.

**1**   Right-click the grade 1 bar for the last doorway shot in the sequence.

**2**   Choose Reset Grade 1 from the shortcut menu.

All settings in all rooms are reset to their default values.

This resets only the one instance of the clip. If you want to reset the grade for all items in the group, use the newly reset grade to do so.

**3**  Drag the grade 1 on the last clip to the group icon in the Shots tab in the Setup room.

> **NOTE** ▶ You can safely ignore the Grade Copy Error. It's simply informing you that you're trying to copy a "blank" grade.

Grade 1 is now reset for all instances of that clip, including the first instance, from which you dragged the settings to the group in the first place.

Be aware that this operation is not undoable.

Color's grade management tools make short work of the complex job colorists face when dealing with real-world projects that include many similar or identical shots in the course of each sequence.

Because you can save and restore grades within a session using the memory banks, or across sessions using saved grade and correction files, you never have to recreate looks from scratch. This not only saves you time, but ensures consistency across your whole show.

## Lesson Review

1.  How many grades can each clip contain?

2.  Can you duplicate a grade on a single clip?

3.  Where are saved corrections and grades stored?

4.  How do you switch between grades on a single clip?

5.  How do you delete a grade?

6.  Do corrections contain grades or do grades contain corrections?

7.  What does an orange grade bar in the grade track mean?

8.  Can clips be grouped in the Timeline?

9.  How do you remove a clip from a group?

10. True or false: Modifying one clip's grade in a group automatically updates the rest of the clips in that group.

### Answers

1.  Each clip has four possible grades.

2.  You can effectively duplicate a grade by copying and pasting—or dragging—from one grade to another.

3.  Home > Library > Application Support > Color, and then in individual folders for each type of saved setting.

4.  By selecting the grade number in the menu or Timeline, or by pressing Control + the grade number.

5.  Right-click the grade and choose Remove Grade from the shortcut menu.

6.  Grades contain corrections.

7.  Orange indicates the user-selected *beauty grade*.

8.  No.

9.  Right-click and drag from the name to an empty space in the Shots browser.

10. False.

**6**

Lesson Files     Color Book Files > Lesson Files > Lesson 06 > ColorFX.colorproj

Time     This lesson takes approximately 75 minutes to complete.

Goals     Add individual nodes to create special effects

Combine nodes to create unique or custom looks

Understand node-based effects flows

Save node trees as preset effects

Reapply saved presets to other clips

Apply and customize preset effects

Learn how to deconstruct a preset

# Lesson 6
# Color Effects

If you're like most colorists, the more comfortable you grow with manipulating the various aspects of an image, the more likely it is that you'll start dreaming of the unlimited possibilities of such manipulation. Color correction can mean so much more than fixing skin tones and creating beautiful sunsets. You can make radical changes to your footage, not only affecting mood and tone, but changing the story itself.

From transforming footage that was shot during the day to appear as if it was shot at night, to creating period looks, to simulating various film acquisition, processing, and presentation techniques, Color can facilitate a wide range of effects that greatly expand your ability to tell your story more effectively.

## Using the Color Effects Room

Color has a special place to build and explore such effects; a playground where you can combine and manipulate a set of building blocks that affect your images in myriad ways. The building blocks are called *nodes* and the playground is the Color Effects room (or *Color FX* room).

Nearly all of the elements in the Color Effects room could be replicated through sophisticated manipulations in the Primary or Secondaries rooms, but in many instances it's far quicker and simpler to apply a pre-baked color effect and adjust a few parameters instead.

**1**   Open Lesson Files > Lesson 06 > **Color_FX.colorproj.**

**2**   Choose File > Reconnect Media and navigate to Lesson Files > Lesson 06 > Media, then click Choose.

**3**   Press the spacebar to play the first clip (**SHOT01_HOUSE.mov**).

The clip shows a simple tilt revealing a white house.

**NOTE ▶** The Color FX room uses the results of the Primary In and Secondaries rooms, so any corrections applied in those rooms will be visible when viewing a clip in the Color FX room.

Using the effects in the Color FX room, you can quickly make radical changes to the look of the shot and, by extension, to the feel of the show.

**4**   Click the Color FX tab (or press Command-4) to open the Color Effects room.

The Color FX room is divided into four main areas: On the left, the Node List displays all the available effects. The middle area, where you construct your custom effects by dragging and connecting various nodes, is called the Node View. The right side has two tabs: Parameters, where you set the values for each node, and the Color FX bin, which contains a collection of preset node trees that perform specific effects.

## Applying Nodes

There are several different types of nodes. Some apply specific effects, such as adding blur or noise to an image. Some allow you to limit how other nodes are applied. For example, a node may allow you to apply an effect to just the red channel, or to a masked area of the image, or to only one field of interlaced footage. Other nodes affect how different components are combined, so if you have a masked area with one effect on it, and the rest of the image has a different effect, you can choose to recombine the two areas using different blending modes. Finally, there are nodes that perform these recombinations, so if you've separated, say, the red, green, and blue channels to perform discrete effects in each channel, there are nodes to put the image back together.

> **TIP** ▶ For a detailed description of each node and how to use it, consult the Color User Manual.

Applying individual nodes to a clip is simple, and sometimes one node may be all you need to create the desired effect.

> **NOTE** ▶ An Output node is required in order for any effect to be rendered.

1 Double-click the Blur node in the Node List.

The Blur node appears in the Node View, and its effect is applied to the clip. The amount of blur is controlled by the settings in the Parameters tab.

2 Click the Parameters tab (if that tab isn't already showing).

3 Middle-click the Spread parameter and drag to the right to increase the blur amount to 3.

Although simply blurring an entire image this way is not common or practical, this node can be an essential element of more complex effects, such as softening skin tones to create a more glamorous portrait-type look. If you don't like an effect, nodes are easy to delete.

**4** Select the Blur node in the Node View and press Delete to remove the node.

## Building Color Effects

Individual nodes can be useful, but the real power of the Color FX room emerges when you combine multiple nodes to create more complex effects. In this next section you'll construct a hand-drawn look.

**1** Drag the Duotone node to the Node View.

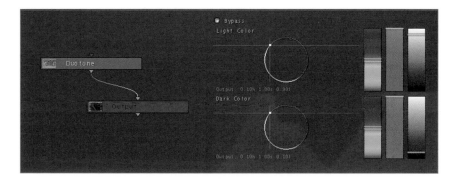

When you drag a node instead of double-clicking it, the node is added and, as a bonus, an Output node is added as well. The two are connected by a white line commonly called a noodle.

The Output node is required in order for Color to incorporate your effect into the render pipeline. It is the result of the Output that gets sent to the Geometry room. Any nodes not connected to the Output node will be ignored.

**2**    In the Parameters tab, customize the colors of your duotone effect.

**3**    Double-click the Edge Detector node to add it to your Node View.

Whichever node is selected determines what is displayed in the Viewer and which parameters are displayed in the Parameters tab.

**4**    Click the Duotone node, then click the Edge Detector node again. Notice that the Viewer updates to display the effect of each node as you select it.

Because no noodles connect the two nodes, you can see only one effect or the other. To combine their effects, you must create a noodle to join them.

Each node has small triangular Input and Output ports on its top and bottom edges. You can control how the various nodes interact by the way these ports are connected.

**5**    Drag the Output port on the bottom of the Duotone node to the Input port on the Edge Detector node.

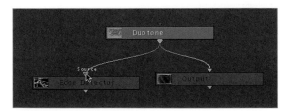

**TIP** ▶ You must release the mouse button only after the Input port lights up. Otherwise the noodle will not successfully link the two nodes.

The nodes are connected with a noodle, but you'll notice that your Viewer only shows the duotone effect. Clicking the Output port selected that node, so even though the two nodes are connected, you're only monitoring the selected node.

**6**  Click the Edge Detector node to select it.

Because the nodes are now connected, the Edge Detector node now displays the combined effect of the two nodes. The duotone is applied first, and the edge detector after that.

**7**  Click the Input port on the top of the Edge Detector node.

This disconnects the nodes, and the Viewer now displays the edge detector without the duotone effect.

**NOTE** ▶ Notice that when you move your pointer over a node's Input port, a tiny display indicates the source currently feeding that node.

**8**   Drag a noodle from the Output port of the Duotone node to the Input port of the Edge Detector node to reconnect them.

**9**   Click the Output node.

The Output node shows only the duotone effect, because even though the edge detector is visible in the node tree and connected to the duotone effect, it isn't connected to the Output node. The Output node controls the final result of the Color FX room, so leaving a node disconnected from it means that node won't actually be included in the final render of this shot.

**10**   Drag a noodle from the Output port of the Edge Detector node to the Input port on the Output node.

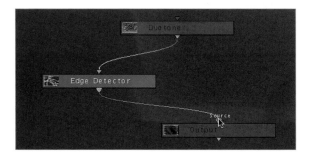

Each Input port can accept only one source, so by dragging the edge detector to the Output node, you replace the noodle from the Duotone node.

**NOTE** ► Some nodes do accept multiple sources. Such nodes contain more than one Input port.

## Controlling Node Order

The nodes in your Node View construct a sort of flowchart. The image goes in at the top and comes out on the bottom. The noodles connecting the nodes' inputs and outputs determine the order in which the effects are applied. This order can have a significant impact on the resulting image. For example, currently the duotone is feeding the edge detector, but what would happen if you reversed that order?

**1**   Drag the Output port of the edge detector to the Input port of the duotone.

Color won't let you make this link, because you can't create circular references in your node trees.

**2**   Click the Input port on the edge detector to disconnect the Duotone node.

**3**   Now, repeat step 1.

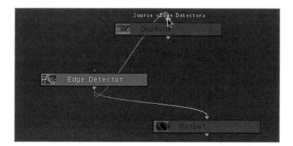

The output of the edge detector becomes the source of the duotone.

**TIP** Although not required, it's helpful to drag your nodes in a way that lets you easily understand the natural flow of data from one node to the next. In this case, moving the Edge Detector node above the Duotone node makes the whole node tree easier to understand.

You can lasso around multiple nodes to select more than one at a time to move them or even delete them.

**4**   Drag the nodes to rearrange them and tidy up your Node View.

**5**   Drag a noodle from the Output port of the Duotone node to the Input port of the Output node.

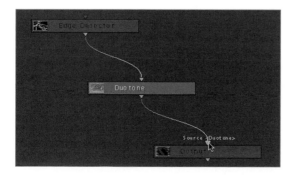

**6** Click the Output node to make it active.

By reordering the nodes, you can create two different looks. In one case, the edge detection is applied to the duotone, and in the other, the duotone is applied to the edge detection.

Duotone First                    Edge Detector First

**7** Click the Duotone node.

**8** Lower the contrast slider of the light color and raise the contrast slider for the dark color of the Duotone node.

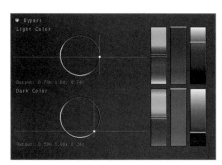 

Because the edge detector turns edges white and the rest of the image black, and the duotone allows you to set a color for the lightest and darkest areas of the image, this combined effect allows you to create a custom type of edge detection, where you can customize the colors of the edges and the flat areas.

**Bypassing Nodes**

Occasionally, you may want to temporarily disable a node to observe how that one element is affecting your overall effect. Each node has a bypass checkbox that allows you to turn off the effect without resetting the parameters.

1    Select a node and click the Bypass checkbox at the top of the Parameters tab.

This disables the effect of that node.

2    Deselect the Bypass checkbox to reactivate the node.

## Monitoring Inactive Nodes

The selected node determines which effect is displayed in the Viewer and which settings are accessible in the Parameters tab. However, sometimes you may want to monitor one node while changing parameters on another. For example, you may want to make an adjustment to the edge detection scale while observing the output of the duotone. This lets you see how one node affects another later in the chain.

1    Double-click the Duotone node.

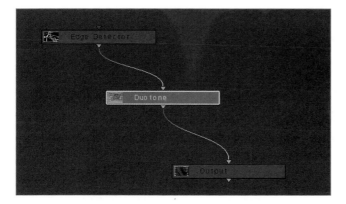

The node turns beige. This indicates that it's controlling the display in the Viewer. By default, it also activates the node, so its parameters are displayed in the Parameters tab.

**2** Single-click the Edge Detector node.

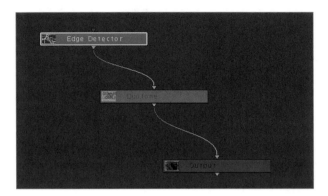

The node turns blue, and the controls in the Parameter tab are updated, but the Viewer continues to display the output of the beige node.

Now you can adjust the edge detection settings while observing how they affect the combined effect of the two nodes.

**3** Set the Scale parameter to 10, and the Bias to -.05.

This smoothes out the edge detection, and the combined effect results in a clean line-drawing effect.

**4** Double-click any empty spot in the Node View area to deselect the beige node.

## Adding Nodes to Existing Trees

Once you've begun building a node tree, you can add new effects without disconnecting and reconnecting all your noodles.

1   Drag the Maximum node to the noodle connecting the Duotone node to the Output node. When the noodle turns blue, release the mouse button.

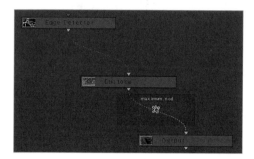

The node is inserted between the two existing nodes, automatically connected to both. It is also automatically made active.

2   Increase the brush size parameter to about 1.25.

This parameter fattens the lines, increasing the hand-drawn look of the effect.

Finally, you can mix the results of this hand-drawn effect back in with the original image in a number of ways.

3   Drag a Blend node onto the noodle between the Maximum and Output nodes.

4   Adjust the Blend parameter to your liking (here, we've set it to about .75).

The Blend node has two inputs and simply mixes the two images together based on the value in the Blend parameter.

When you added the node to the tree, the Maximum node was automatically plugged into Input 1, and Input 2 was left at the default. Any input without a noodle defaults to the source image with no effects applied, so in this case you're mixing the results of your effect with the original image. You could conceivably build another branch of nodes and plug that into Input 2 to create an even more complex tree.

**TIP** ▶ Instead of mixing the affected image with the original using the Blend node, try one of the other compositing nodes such as Add, Multiply, Lighten, Darken, or Difference. Each will produce a different result.

As you can see, creating color effects using node trees is both easy and fun. You'll likely employ a fair amount of trial and error as you learn the uses of the various nodes, and soon you'll be creating your own complex effects with multiple branches and more nodes than you can imagine.

## Saving and Reapplying Effects as Presets

Now that you've created a masterpiece, you probably want to apply the same effect to every clip in your show. Perhaps you may even want to save it to apply to clips in other shows, or to email to your friends to prove just how bright a colorist you are.

Fortunately, Color allows you to save and reapply Color Effects settings in exactly the same way you saved and reused Primary and Secondary corrections in Lesson 5.

First of all, the Timeline displays a bar in the grade track indicating the Color FX correction applied to the clip.

**NOTE** ▶ Sometimes Color's Timeline doesn't update automatically to show the grades applied to a clip. To force the Timeline to redraw, select a different clip or a different grade, then switch back to the clip or grade you're working with.

This can be copied or dragged to other clips just like other corrections. For more information on copying corrections from one clip to another, please see Lesson 5, "Grade Management."

Additionally, you can save your color effects to a file that can be reapplied to other clips in any Color project on any Color system.

**1**   Click the Color FX Bin tab.

**2**   Click the Icon view button to see a preview of each effect.

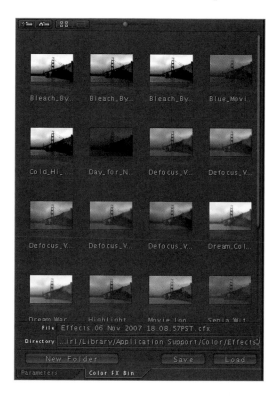

The Color FX bin is very similar to the file viewer in the Primary In and Secondaries rooms. The only differences are that it's populated with preset effects, and that it's on the right side of the room instead of the left.

For now, you'll ignore the existing presets, and save your own.

**3**   In the File field, type *Indigo Hand-Drawn Look.* Click Save.

The custom preset is saved and appears among the other presets in the window.

**4**    Click the Directory field to see a pop-up revealing the folder on the disk where the effect file was saved.

By default it's saved in Home > Library > Application Support > Color > Effects folder.

**NOTE ▶** If you select a different folder when clicking the Directory field, you can always return to the home folder by clicking the Home button at the top of the Color FX bin.

**5**    In the Timeline, press the Down Arrow to move to the next clip (**04_WARPLANE.mov**).

**6**    Locate the Indigo Hand-Drawn Look preset, and double-click it or drag it to the Node View.

The saved effect is applied to the new clip.

## Modifying an Applied Preset

In this case, the outline appears a little too thick around the plane, and the blend mix is a bit too high. Once the effect is applied to your new clip, you can modify the individual parameters however you like. The saved preset will not be affected.

**1**    Double-click the Output node so your Viewer always displays the finished image.

**2**   Click the Maximum node.

**3**   Click the Parameters tab to access the Maximum parameters.

**4**   Click the Bypass checkbox to disable this node.

**5**   Click the Blend node.

**6**   Lower the Blend parameter to .25.

These settings are only a suggestion. Feel free to experiment to create different effects and different combinations. Add or remove nodes as you see fit. If at some point you come up with a new effect you'd like to save, return to the Presets bin, type a name for your effect, and click Save.

## Working with Preset Color Effects

Color ships with a collection of very useful and versatile preset color effects. Some are simple two- or three-node combinations with a few well-chosen parameter settings. Others are complex monstrosities that many colorists would be loath to build themselves.

In either case, applying them couldn't be easier.

1   In the Color FX bin, switch to List View.

2   Double-click the Bleach_Bypass_Adjustable preset.

    **NOTE** ▶ Applying a new preset replaces any nodes currently in the Node View.

The preset is applied to the clip.

3   In the Node View, double-click the Output node to display it in the Viewer.

4   Single-click the Saturation node to access its parameters.

5   Click the Parameters tab.

6   Adjust the Saturation parameter to 1.

This adds a bit more color to the airplane without overriding the general effect. Any of the nodes can be adjusted this way to customize and finesse the effect to the needs of your particular shot.

▶ **What Is Bleach Bypass?**

Bleach bypass is the photographic technique of skipping the step in the development process that usually removes the silver from the film. This effectively renders a black-and-white version of the image on top of the color image, albeit in an organic, integrated way. (Technicolor's ENR and Deluxe Labs' ACE are proprietary variants of this technique which allow the film to be only partially bleached.)

The resulting images typically have increased contrast and grain and lowered saturation, especially in certain hues. This creates a harsh, cool, metallic look that has been wildly overused in recent years in commercials, television shows, music videos, and even feature films (such as *Saving Private Ryan, Three Kings, Fight Club*, and so on).

Projects intending to employ this process typically make adjustments during production to retain extra detail in the bright areas (by underexposing slightly) and increase saturation (typically through production design and film-stock choices), as the process generally blows out whites and removes saturation. If your source footage wasn't shot with this intention, you may find the results undesirable (or you may have to deliberately step down various parameter values to achieve the desired result).

Despite its overuse, the look remains remarkably popular, so you can count on clients requesting it for many years to come. Fortunately, Color provides several simulated varieties of the effect as presets, so you can be trendy without breaking a sweat.

**Analyzing Presets**

There are several other bleach bypass presets for you to experiment with. Naturally, different footage will respond to the filters differently, and your desired result may require further manipulation of the various parameters.

1   Click the Color FX Bin tab.

2   Double-click the Warm_glo preset.

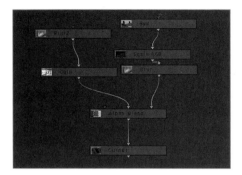 

The Bleach_Bypass_Adjustable preset is replaced with the Warm Glo effect.

The Color FX room is particularly useful for glow effects, which are another of the most popular types of effects that fall in the colorist's domain. Glows typically require the application of some blur to at least portions of the image, and there are no glow functions in the Primary or Secondaries rooms.

To see how this particular effect is created, you can view each step of the process by clicking on the nodes in the tree. It's helpful to start at the bottom.

3   Click the Alpha Blend node.

This node takes three inputs, combining the first two based on the transparency defined by the third. This means that the image feeding into Input 3 is only used as a grayscale matte to limit which portions of Input 2 are visible.

Input 1 is empty, which means it automatically takes a clean copy of the video, so the nodes feeding into Input 2 are being mixed with the clean video.

4   Click the Gain node.

This is the blurred version of the image. The Gain node is used to add the "warm" color that gives this preset its name.

5   Click the Blur2 node.

This node shows the blurred version before the color effect is added.

Next, examine the matte.

**6** Click the B&W node.

This takes a copy of the original video and strips the chrominance. Mattes work by making black areas transparent (you'll see the version from Input 1), white areas opaque (you'll see the version from Input 2), and gray areas semi-transparent (you'll see a mix of both).

By creating a black-and-white version of the image, you create a mask based on the contrast of the image itself. However, the image is mostly gray, so to make the matte have a clear edge, you must bifurcate the gray values, creating a high-contrast version.

**7** Click the Scale RGB node.

This node does just that, making the plane itself opaque, while the sky is transparent.

**8**  Click the Blur node.

This node adds a bit of softness to the matte, so the edge between Input 1 and Input 2 is gradual. The amount of this blur (combined with the blur in the other branch) controls the amount of apparent "glow" in the final image.

**9**  Click again on the Alpha Blend node.

By understanding the components that make up an effect like this, you can more effectively customize them or even create your own versions of similar effects.

### Observing Bypassed Nodes

Every node has a Bypass checkbox that allows you to temporarily examine how an effect looks when one of the nodes is removed from the tree, without having to delete the node or reset its parameters.

For example, let's say you liked almost everything about this glow effect, but didn't like the "warming" effect created by the Gain node.

**1**  Double-click the Output node to view the final result of the effect.

**2**  Click the Gain node to access its parameters.

**3** In the Parameters tab, select the Bypass checkbox.

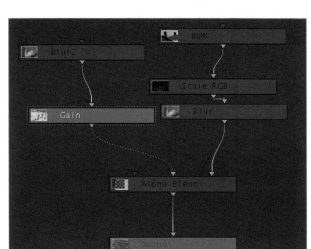

The Gain node is ignored, and a dotted orange outline surrounds the node and its noodles to indicate this in the Node View.

**TIP** ▸ This is another useful way to see how each node is contributing to the final result. By viewing the output, and turning the Bypass checkbox on and off for each of the other nodes, you can observe the effect of each node.

Although the presets provided with Color are powerful effects that can be used in a wide range of circumstances, you should always look at them as a starting point, or a suggested recipe. By customizing them or recreating similar effects tailored to your specific needs, you can quickly create masterful effects that are truly unique.

Best of all, you can save your creations and share them with other Color users. And finally, it's a good idea to get involved in one of the many online forums where colorists share tips and swap color FX scripts. Before you know it, you'll have more preset effects than you know what to do with!

## Lesson Review

1. What is a node?

2. What is a noodle?

3. How do you customize a node?

4. True or false: Changing node order has no effect.

5. How can you monitor one node, and modify another?

6. What happens if an Input port is empty?

7. Can an Input port have more than one source?

8. Can nodes be added between existing nodes?

9. How can a node tree be saved?

10. What happens to existing nodes when a preset is applied?

### *Answers*

1. An individual effect element.

2. A line indicating the flow of data from node to node.

3. By changing settings in the Parameters tab.

4. False. Node order is critical to achieving desired results.

5. Double-click the node you want to view, then single-click the node you want to modify.

6. The source image is used as the input.

7. No. A node requiring more than one input will have multiple Input ports.

8. Yes, by dragging directly to the noodle that connects them.

9. Node trees can be saved as preset effects in the Color FX bin.

10. All existing nodes are replaced.

# 7

**Lesson Files**  Color Book Files > Lesson Files > Lesson 07 > Color_Lesson07.colorproj

**Time**  This lesson takes approximately 60 minutes to complete.

**Goals**  Create a *Black Hawk Down/Mogadishu* look

Create a *CSI Miami* look

Create a *Schindler's List* color isolation look

Create a flashback/dream look

Create a "Saturated Sunrise" look

Build a skin diffusion Color FX from scratch

# Common Recipes

Now it's time to have some fun and mimic the masters. In addition to coming up with your own color effects, there are times when you may want to "borrow" someone else's signature look—drawn, perhaps, from a specific film or a genre of films. In this lesson, we've put together recipes for some useful and interesting looks you might be familiar with, along with some handy techniques for dealing with skin tone correction. (Please note that all of these looks were created with Broadcast Safe on.)

Let's start cooking!

## *Black Hawk Down/Mogadishu* **Look**

Our aim here is to turn some fairly flat-looking HD footage into a typical Hollywood depiction of "Africa." This footage was shot in Rwanda, so we aren't trying to fake the location. We're merely trying to produce an image that will look familiar to audiences who, through long exposure to television and film, have come to associate a certain film look with that continent.

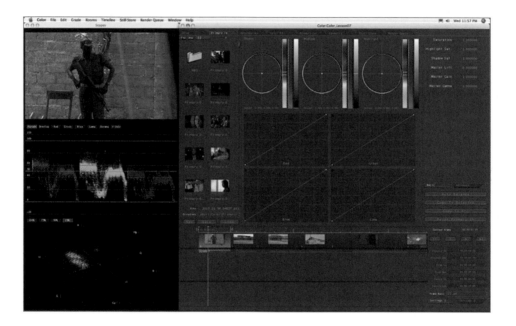

1    Open Lesson Files > Lesson 07 > **Color_Lesson07.colorproj**.

There are nine shots in the Timeline grouped into a Before section at left, and an After section at right. We'll start with the first one, showing a security guard holding an AK-47 machine gun.

2    Choose File > Reconnect Media and navigate to Lesson Files > Lesson 07 > Media, then click Choose.

3    Right-click (or Control-click) the Timeline ruler and drag to zoom in on the first few clips.

We're starting fresh with this shot; no initial corrections have been made.

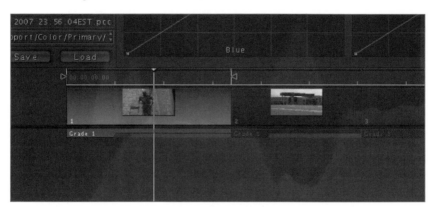

4   Press Command-2 to activate the Primary In room.

5   To make sure your clip is active, double-click it.

The next step is to increase the overall contrast of the clip, using Luma in the Waveform Monitor as a guide.

6   First, use the Highlight contrast slider to increase the highlights by approximately 15%.

7   Then, using the Shadow contrast slider, reduce the black level to about 1% black until the highlights touch 100% in the Waveform Monitor.

Again, using the Waveform Monitor as a guide, be careful not to crush the shadows too much initially.

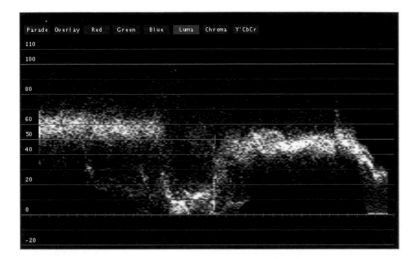

**8** In the Basic tab on the right of frame, next to the color balance controls, type *0.9* in the Saturation field to reduce the saturation to 0.90.

**9** Press Command-3 to open the Secondaries room, and click Secondaries tab 1 (if it isn't already active).

**10** Select the Enabled checkbox to enable the first Secondary (S1).

**11** Using the Midtone color balance control, slowly introduce a yellow tone across the entire image.

> **NOTE ▶** The exact amount of yellow you add is your choice, but be careful not to push it too far or it will overpower the final look you're going for.

**12** Next, we need to reduce saturation in the shadows. In the Basic tab next to the color balance controls, reduce Shadow Saturation to 0.30.

**13** Click Secondaries tab 2. Use the secondary Sat Curve to increase the warmer tones and reduce the blues and aquas, until your Sat Curve resembles the one shown here.

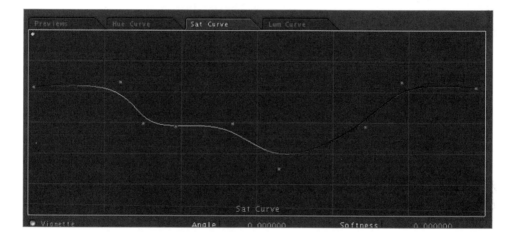

**14** Select and deselect the Enabled checkbox while watching the Vectorscope to see the impact of this secondary correction.

**15** Press Command-5 to bring up the Primary Out room.

### Increasing Color Density

Now we'll manipulate the secondary curves to increase the density of the colors. Use the image below as reference for adjusting the secondary curves to achieve the desired look.

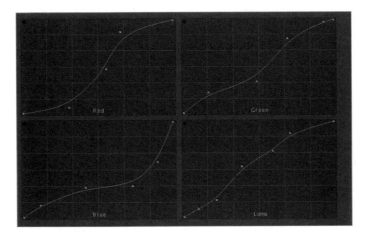

1   Toggle the grade on and off by pressing Control-G to compare the original shot with the graded one.

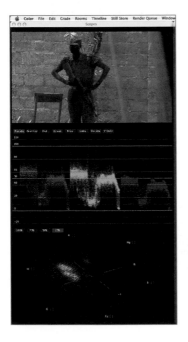

**2**   The next step is to make slight tweaks in the Primary Out Room to ensure that you don't crush (lower) the shadow levels too much. Otherwise, you'll be in danger of losing the image detail in both the shadows and darker midtones.

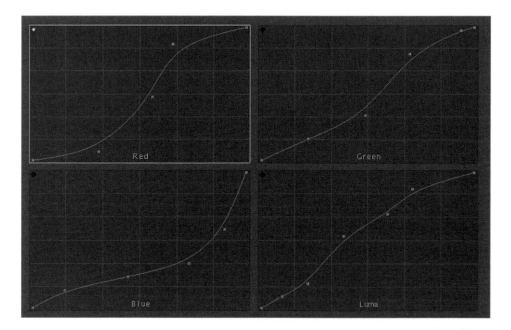

**TIP**   After you've established this look you could drag this grade to other clips (as shown below), but another easy way is to save this look as a grade in the Setup room that you can then reuse later. Additionally, you could use groups, as discussed in Lesson 5, to make applying this grade to comparable clips even easier.

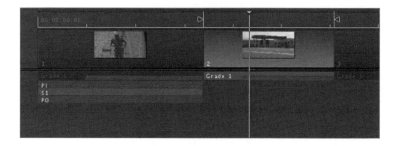

## *CSI Miami* Look

Now it's time to make a fairly overcast day in Sydney look like a warm, cloud-free day in Miami. We also have a vintage car in the shot, which we'll dress up to help make the scene look more convincing.

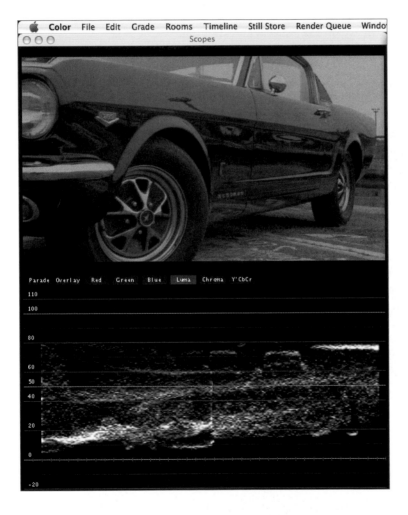

1   Proceed to shot 3 (**03CITYCAR**) on the Timeline.

2   Press Command-2 to make the Primary In room active. Double-click the clip to ensure that it's active.

**3**  The next step is to boost the overall contrast of the clip. First, move the playhead in the Timeline past the halfway mark in the clip until the frame you see matches the image below. Next, increase the highlights by approximately 95% white using the Highlight Slider, and then reduce the black level to about 1% using the Shadows slider, being careful not to crush the shadows too much initially.

At all times, keep an eye on the Waveform Monitor as your guide.

4 Increase the saturation to 1.33 by typing *1.33* in the Saturation field or middle-clicking and dragging until you reach the desired value.

5 Press Command-3 to open the Secondaries room.

6 Click Secondaries tab 1 (if it isn't already active).

7 Select the Enabled and Vignette checkboxes.

8 Choose a square vignette and stretch it out in the preview area until it covers the top 20% of the screen.

**9**  Type *0.8* in the Softness field. If necessary, toggle the Control pull-down to ensure that you're switched to Inside control.

**10**  Ensure that you are set to Final View in the Secondaries preview area, and push the Midtone color balance control into the orange-red direction until your clip resembles the screen below.

> **NOTE** ► Be careful when adjusting the midtones. Because you're working with Broadcast Safe on, if you push the midtones too far into the orange-reds, the color will clip.

**11**  Click Secondaries tab 2.

We now need to use the secondary Sat Curve to increase reds, blues, and yellows, and reduce the greens.

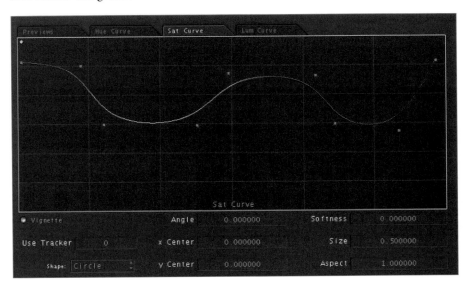

**12** Use the third secondary (S3) to create an additional vignette in the top half of the frame as shown below. Set the vignette shape to Circle and approximate the settings shown in yellow in the screenshot.

Next, we'll bring down the outside shadow levels to darken the road.

**13** Ensure that the control pull-down is set to Outside, and use the Shadow contrast slider to crush the shadows by about 19–22%.

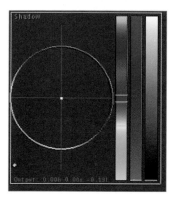

### Using Your Grade on a New Clip

Now it's time to move on to the next clip and drag the entire grade over. We'll try to modify this look for the building. Initially, it looks good, but to be safe, let's rotate the "grad" (as in gradient) in the sky.

> **NOTE ►** Gradient filters (grads) are thin layers of glass used by cinematographers and DPs around the world to filter light frequency out of an image prior to acquisition to film or digital. Only recently have tools like Color allowed us to simulate this effect digitally by positioning square vignettes in a frame, like dropping a glass grad in front of a camera lens. Camera matte boxes allow an operator to rotate glass grads. In Color, we can simulate this effect by rotating a vignette.

It's very common to start with a base grade that generally works and then copy this to all the clips that are similar in framing. You can then proceed to each shot independently and make minor tweaks without affecting the neighbors on the Timeline, as you'll do now.

**1**    Press the Down Arrow key to move to shot 4.

In this shot the sky is pretty flat and cool. You can warm it up quite a bit by going back to the Secondaries room and using the adjustments from the previous clip and tweaking them slightly.

**2** Drag grade 1 from shot 3 (**03CITYCAR**) and drop on grade 1 of shot 4 (**04CITYFACTORY**).

**3** Increase the reds and saturation in the sky, adjusting the color balance controls as shown below.

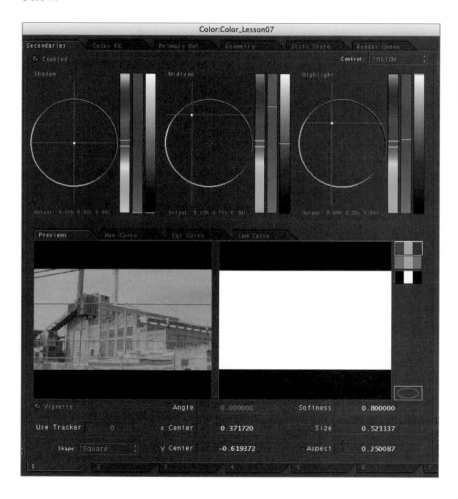

**4** Increase the softness so that the sky gradient is not too over the top.

**5** Toggle Control-G to compare the graded image to the original.

## *Schindler's List* **Look**

You can create an interesting look by simply reducing the color levels in the image and relying on just black, white, and a single color hue. This popular effect was perhaps used most memorably in Steven Spielberg's *Schindler's List*, to draw attention to a girl's red coat in an otherwise black-and-white setting during the liquidation of the Krakow ghetto. In this exercise, we'll recreate the effect using a shot of a prisoner in a cell, as shown below (this is the final version—yours should look like this at the end of the exercise).

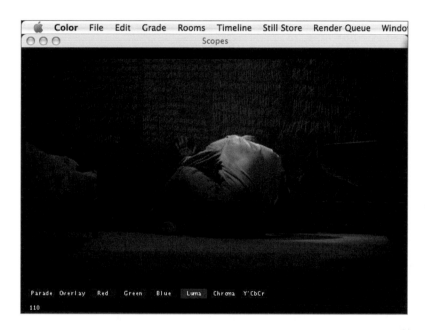

**1**    Proceed to shot 5 (**Jail**) on the Timeline, and double-click it to make it active.

**2**    Press Command-2 to make the Primary In room active.

**3**    Next, boost the overall contrast of the clip by increasing the highlights by approximately 10%, and reducing the black level to about 5% black using the Waveform Monitor as a guide. Use the the shadow and highlight sliders to make these adjustments.

We still need black detail for this shot.

**4**   Press Command-3 to open the Secondaries room.

**5**   Click Secondaries tab 1 (if it isn't already active).

**6**   Click the eyedropper, and in the Viewer, drag the red crosshairs across the figure's orange jumpsuit. The eyedropper should auto-enable the Secondary.

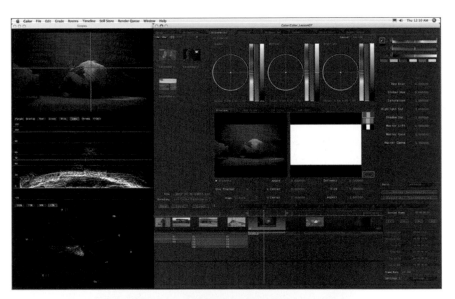

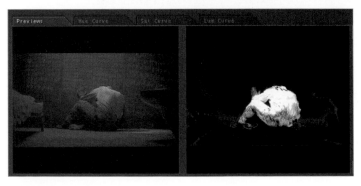

**7** Now you'll improve the key by extending the tolerance handles outward to feather the edges and setting the Key Blur to 3.0.

**8** Continue to enhance the matte using the HSL qualifiers, adjusting them so the settings resemble the screen below.

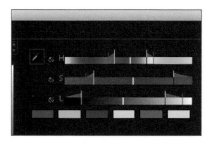

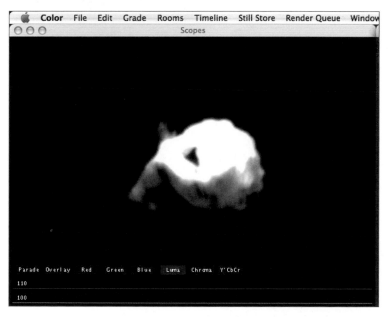

**9** If necessary, check the Control pull-down to ensure that you're switched to Inside control, and then proceed to move all the color balance controls toward orange.

**10** Toggle the Control pull-down to select the outside controls of the key and then reduce the saturation to 0.

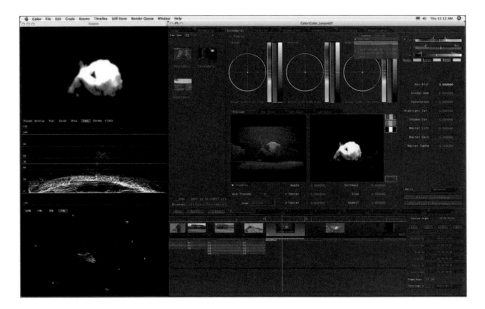

Now let's add more contrast to the black-and-white walls.

**11** Using the shadow and highlight contrast sliders, reduce the shadows by 12% and increase the highlights by 40%.

**12** Click Secondaries tab 2.

The next step is to create a vignette and give the lighting more downward direction.

**13** Enable the Vignette checkbox and select a circle vignette. Place the circle around the man and soften the edges.

In the next few steps you'll try to create a pool of light on him, similar to that of a downward-facing lamp.

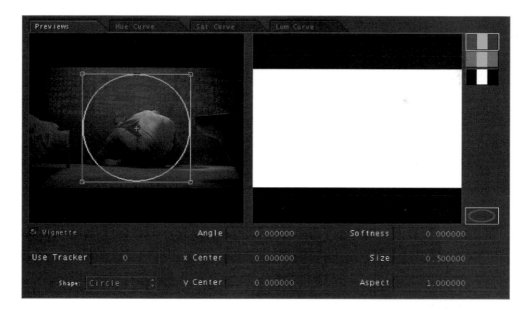

**14** Switch to Outside control using the Control pull-down; then reduce the shadows by a further 15%. If it looks too harsh, increase the softness of the vignette using the Softness field.

**15** Now compare before and after!

# Flashback Look

Since the first "talkies," soft-focus effects have been used to evoke flashbacks, dream sequences, and romantic moments that occur somehow outside of everyday time. In this exercise, we'll give a fallen chandelier the full '40s flashback treatment.

**1**   Proceed to shot 6 (**EmptyHouse**) on the Timeline.

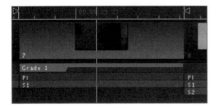

**2**   Press Command-2 to make the Primary In room active, and double-click the clip to make sure that it's active.

3   Increase the overall contrast of the clip using the Luma curve. Plot the points as
    shown below.

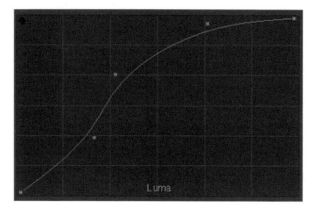

4   Press Command-3 to open the Secondaries room.

5   Click Secondaries tab 1 (if it isn't already active).

6   Advance the playhead until you are in the middle of the shot as pictured below.

7   Click the eyedropper, and in the Viewer, drag the red crosshairs across the white windows.

Your key should look like the image below.

**8**  Now extend the key by deselecting the H (Hue) and S (Saturation) sliders. Shift-click the left range handle of the Lightness slider and drag it to the left to feather.

**9**  Set your Key Blur to 9.0.

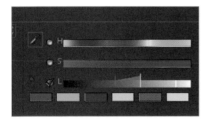

**10**  Make sure you have Inside control selected and push the highlight levels to 2.671 and the shadows to 0.51.

**11**  Increase the feather on the Lightness slider by adjusting the tolerance handles until you begin to see a white glow.

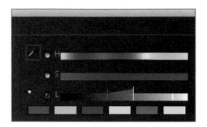 

The key will increase and begin to blow out the highlights.

**NOTE** ▸ It's especially important to have Broadcast Safe on when you're creating this look.

**12** Save the grade for later use.

## Saturated Sunrise Look

"Saturated Sunrise" is an extremely useful effect when the shooting conditions don't measure up to the full drama of the scene. Here we'll take a very flat-looking shot of a World War II plane flying in gray skies and give it a more stylized and saturated look.

1   Select shot 9 in the Timeline, **Warplane**. Right-click the Timeline ruler and drag to zoom in.

2   Press Command-2 to make the Primary In room active, and double-click the clip to make sure it's active.

3   Now it's time to warm up the shot overall by giving the midtones and shadows a healthy orange push as shown below.

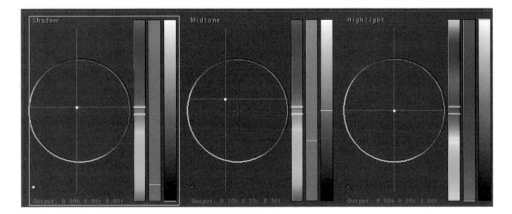

4   Next, create a few points on the Primary Luma curve as shown below.

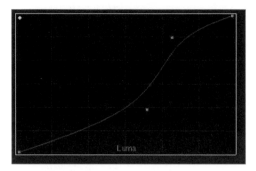

5   Increase the saturation to approximately 1.07-1.1, and then reduce highlight and shadow saturation in the Highlight Sat. and Shadow Sat. fields to 0.92 and 0.9, as shown below.

6   Press Command-3 to open the Secondaries room.

7   Click Secondaries tab 1 and select Enabled.

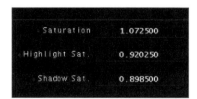

8   Now pull a key using only the Lightness slider in the HSL qualifiers. Follow the screenshots for guidance on settings.

The key should look like the screenshot below.

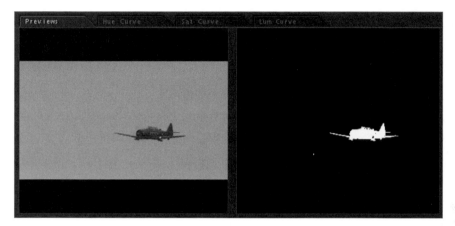

9   Increase the Key Blur to 0.5, select Inside control in the Control pull-down, and then reduce shadow saturation to 0.00.

10   Now proceed to add some green tones to the plane in the midtones.

**11** Click the #2 tab to activate the second secondary to work with the sky.

**12** Select the Enable and Vignette checkboxes and set the Shape pop-up to Circle.

**13** Match the shape settings to those shown in the screenshot below.

**NOTE** ▶ You can switch the Matte Preview mode buttons to Matte Only to see the gradient you've created in the Viewer.

**14** Switch to Outside control mode and add orange tones to the midtones and highlights in this part of the shape, as shown below.

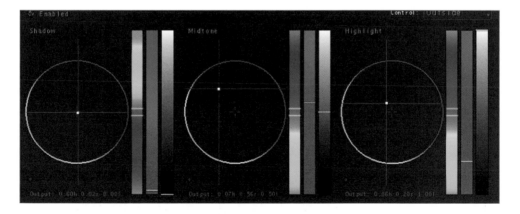

**15** Switch over to Inside control and add blue tones to the shadows, midtones, and highlights.

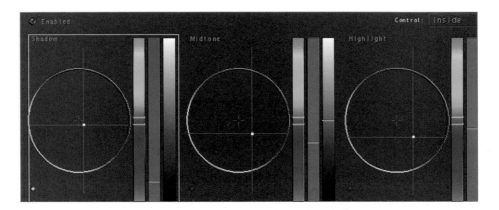

**16** Switch to Final and your image should now look like the screenshot below.

**TIP** ▶ This would be a good time to head to the Color FX room and try some effects presets, especially the bleach bypass looks, on this shot. You should be able to achieve some really great looks by adding Color FX at this stage.

## Skin Diffusion and Beauty Tricks

It's not widely known that colorists spend a good part of their time as digital make-up artists. Films are usually about people, people have skin, and skin—even after the real make-up artist gets through with it—often needs a bit of help. In this exercise, we'll create a skin diffusion effect, one of the most common and useful methods of applying a "digital facial."

1  Proceed to shot 7 (**GirlFace**) on the Timeline.

2  Press Command-2 to make the Primary In room active. Double-click the clip to make sure it's active.

3  Increase the overall contrast of the clip using the Luma curve.

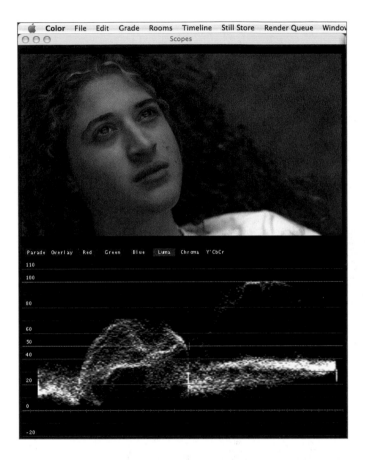

4   Then proceed to warm up the midtones and highlights toward a natural skin tone by dragging the color balance controls until the skin looks nice and healthy.

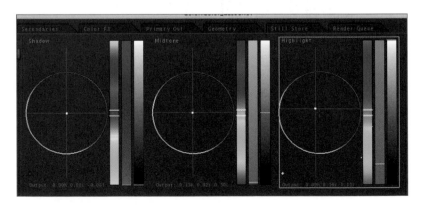

**5**   Press Command-4 to open the Color FX room.

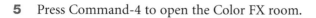

**6**   Now start to drag in Color FX nodes and build a tree as shown in the screenshot below.

**NOTE** ▸ Dragging an effect node to the workspace automatically adds an output node.

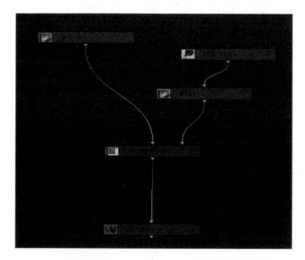

**7**    Once you've built the tree, double-click the HSL Key Node.

**8**    In the Color FX parameters, click the eyedropper and select just the skin tones. Don't worry if you can select it all at first.

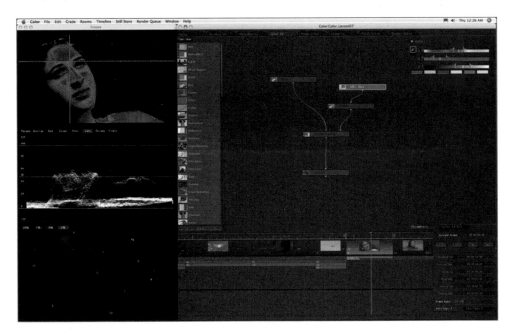

**9**    To blur the key, double-click the Blur node and set the spread to 3.0.

**10** Click the HSL Key once (not twice).

Now you'll be viewing the output of the Blur node, but you'll also be able to change the HSL sliders.

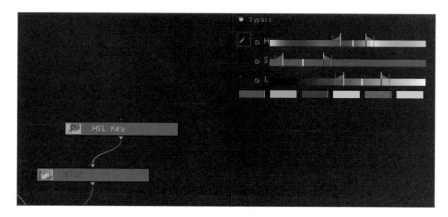

**11** Adjust the sliders around to get a better key as pictured above.

**TIP** ▶ Don't key too much black detail, because we need to keep the eyebrows and eyes sharp to make this look realistic.

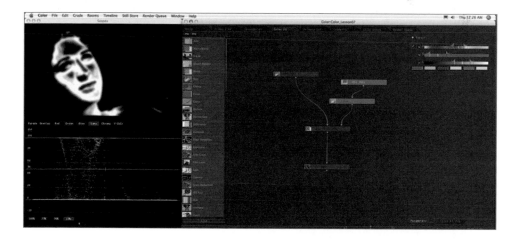

Your key should now look like the screenshot below.

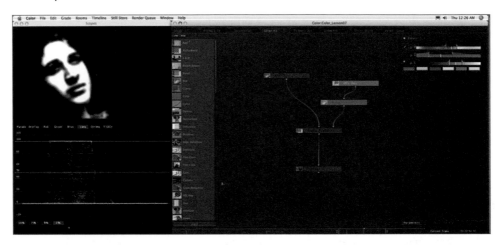

**12** Double-click the Blur 2 node to the left side of the tree and set the spread to 4.0.

**13** Double-click the Output node to see your results.

As you can see, this has made a huge difference.

**14**  Click Control-G to flip back to the original (below) and see how much you've improved the image.

**15**  Drag this grade over to the next shot, which is the same girl in the water.

Switch the grade on and off to see the huge difference the skin diffusion has made. Then enable the grade and hit Play. The whole clip looks great.

Swimmer with skin tone correction

Swimmer (original) without skin tone correction

**16** Save this grade as a preset in the Color FX bin for future use.

## Lesson Review

1. How do you gauge the impact of changes you make to the Sat. Curve to warm up the tones of an image?

2. True or false: If you push the midtones too far into the orange-reds, the color in your image will clip.

3. When using the vignette controls to create a pool of light around a portion of an image, how can you correct when the light becomes too harsh?

4. How can you preview a gradient you've created in the Viewer?

5. True or false: During postproduction, colorists sometimes perform the same tasks that make-up artists do during production.

*Answers*

1. Select and deselect the Enabled checkbox while watching the Vectorscope.

2. True—if Broadcast Safe is on.

3. Increase the softness of the vignette using the Softness field.

4. By enabling the Matte Only button, the third button in the Matte Preview Mode controls.

5. True.

# 8

**Lesson Files**  Color Book Files > Lesson Files > Lesson 08 > Keyframing.colorproj

**Time**  This lesson takes approximately 60 minutes to complete.

**Goals**  Create dynamic corrections and effects in any room

Add, delete, move, and navigate to keyframes

Control Color's interpolation methods

Animate user shapes over time to track objects

Finesse animations by adding and removing keyframes

# Keyframing Effects

So far, all of the corrections, grades, and effects you've created in Color have been static—that is, the settings you applied remained constant across the duration of the clip. While this is adequate for many shots, video is a dynamic medium, and just as often there are changes that occur during a shot that require animated adjustments to your settings.

Color allows such changes for nearly every aspect and parameter in the program through a simple and easy-to-understand keyframing mechanism. This means that everything from basic contrast changes in the Primary In room to the shape and size of custom shapes in the Geometry room can change over time to accommodate changes in your video image. Just be aware that curves (in either the Primary or Secondaries rooms) cannot be keyframed.

## Animating Effects in Color

Color's Timeline contains a special track just for viewing and manipulating keyframes. Each room's keyframes appear on the room's own bar, so you can compare their relative positions and align keyframes from different rooms as needed.

The only significant limitation in Color's keyframing architecture is that individual parameters cannot be keyframed independently. Each room stores all of its settings at each keyframe position. However, this is a satisfactory alternative to having individual keyframes for each of the hundreds of parameters in the program. In most cases you're animating only one or two parameters at a time, anyway.

The other tricky aspect of Color's animation system is that the buttons and onscreen controls don't appear until your keyframes have been added. You must use menu items or keyboard shortcuts to add, remove, or manipulate keyframes, so getting started can be a little intimidating. Never fear; once you get started, you'll find animating effects to be one of the easiest and most straightforward aspects of Color's many features.

**1**    Open Lesson Files > Lesson 08 > **Keyframing.colorproj**.

This project contains three clips, each of which can benefit from animating keyframes in different rooms.

**2**    Choose File > Reconnect Media and navigate to Lesson Files > Lesson 08 > Media, then click Choose.

**3**    Play the first clip.

This clip illustrates a very common problem you're likely to encounter in your own footage. As the camera tilts down from the sky to the house, the exposure changes undesirably. The cinematographer set the exposure to be correct for the sky, but that meant it was too dark for the grass. As a result, the house appears unnecessarily dark. This is easily corrected using a few keyframes in the Primary In room.

4   Press the Up Arrow key to make sure the playhead is parked on the first frame of the clip.

5   Press Command-2 to open the Primary In room.

For the sake of the exercise, assume that the look of the image is perfect for the beginning of the shot, but you want to create a gradual change as the camera tilts. Begin by setting a keyframe on the first frame to lock those settings in for that frame.

6   Choose Timeline > Add Keyframe or press Control-9.

A keyframe is added to the clip; it appears in the keyframe track of the Timeline. Because you haven't yet adjusted any settings, the image in the Viewer is unaffected.

7   Move the playhead toward the end of the shot so that you can clearly see the grass at the bottom of the frame.

This is the frame where you'll set your corrections. However, because you want to animate the effect, you must begin by adding a new keyframe.

**8** Press Control-9 to add a new keyframe at this point.

The second keyframe is added to the Timeline.

**NOTE** ▶ Once you add a keyframe in a particular room, you cannot make any other changes to the settings in that room until a new keyframe is added.

**9** Make some adjustments to improve the look of the shot at this frame. Feel free to create your own settings.

In the example pictured below, the Highlight contrast has been increased and the Shadow contrast decreased to improve overall contrast; then the Shadow color balance control has been moved toward green to add some color to the grass, and the Highlight color balance control has been moved toward magenta to prevent that green from affecting the house and sky.

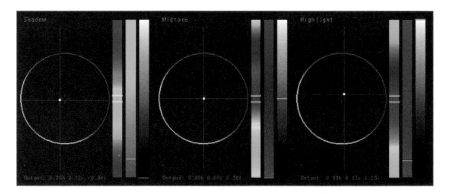

Because you made these changes while parked on a keyframe, the settings are tied to that point in time, and Color will automatically interpolate between the settings on the two keyframes.

**10** Play the clip.

**11** To compare your keyframed corrections with the original clip, press Control-G to disable the grade, and play the clip again.

**12** Press Control-G once again to turn the grade back on.

## Manipulating Keyframes

The Timeline always displays the keyframes for each room, and in the Timeline you can adjust the keyframes' positions and the interpolation method that Color employs to determine the settings on the in-between frames.

> **TIP** Keyframes are saved in the grade in which they were created. Switching to a different grade will update the keyframe track to show the keyframes for that new grade (if any exist).

In most cases, the keyframed effect should be subtle and appear invisible to the viewer. Depending on the specifics of the shot, you may need to finesse the keyframes directly to achieve that subtle effect.

1   Drag the bar beneath the keyframes down to give more room to the keyframe track in the Timeline.

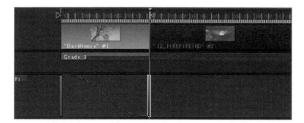

2   Drag the left keyframe to the right within the clip to speed up the animation.

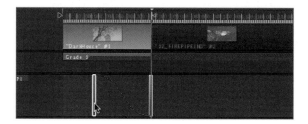

**TIP** ▶ Command-drag a keyframe to see a preview in the Viewer.

3   Play the clip.

By delaying the beginning of the animation, you retain the original settings while the sky is still highly visible in the shot. However, if you move the keyframe too far to the right, the animation happens too quickly and the effect becomes more visible as the shadows take on a slight green cast.

This is a very simple example of keyframing. You can add as many keyframes as you have frames of video in your shot. Any settings that change values from one keyframe to the next will be interpolated for the interim frames.

## Navigating to Keyframes

Once you begin using keyframes, it's important to make sure that you're parked exactly on a keyframe before making additional adjustments. (Color won't let you make any adjustments if you're not parked on a keyframe.) Fortunately, Color provides a quick and easy way to navigate directly to keyframes.

**1**  Right-click (or Control-click) anywhere on the track.

**2**  From the shortcut menu, choose Next Keyframe.

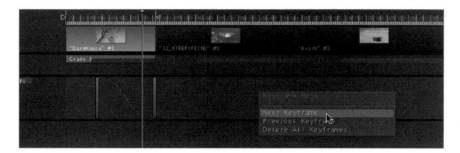

The playhead jumps to the next keyframe for the current clip in the current room.

**TIP** ▸ You can also press Option-Left or the Right Arrow key to navigate to keyframes from the keyboard.

**NOTE** ▸ Keyframes in other rooms or other clips are ignored.

When you're parked on a keyframe, it lights up with a blue highlight. Always check that a keyframe is highlighted before making additional adjustments.

## Deleting Keyframes

If you don't like the results of your animation, you have a variety of possible solutions. First, you can reset the room while parked on a particular keyframe. This allows you to keep your keyframes in place while creating new settings for that particular frame.

Another option is to remove an individual keyframe, which can be helpful when you have many keyframes and want to smooth the interpolation.

**1**  Navigate to the second keyframe.

**2**  Choose Timeline > Remove Keyframe or press Control-0.

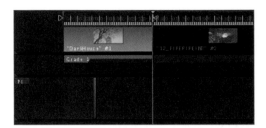

The selected keyframe is deleted, leaving the other keyframe intact. Alternatively, you can just delete all keyframes using the Timeline shortcut menu.

**3**  Press Command-Z to undo step 2.

**4**  Right-click the keyframe track in the Timeline, and choose Delete All Keyframes.

A warning dialog appears asking you to confirm the deletion. This operation cannot be undone, so be careful when choosing this option.

**NOTE ▶** This operation removes only keyframes in the current room.

**5**  Press Cancel to prevent your keyframes from being deleted.

## Keyframing Other Rooms

The basics of keyframing work exactly the same in all of Color's rooms, but it will be helpful to explore some other keyframing examples to familiarize yourself with all of the various settings and controls.

While keyframing can be used to compensate for dynamic exposure or other problems in your source footage, it can also be used to create dramatic and exciting special effects.

**1**  Press the Down Arrow key to move to the second clip.

This is a shot of a flame blowing out of a factory. You can keyframe a Secondary correction to perform a selective desaturation over the duration of the shot.

**2**   Press Command-3 to open the Secondaries room.

**3**   Click the eyedropper and drag across the flame in the Viewer.

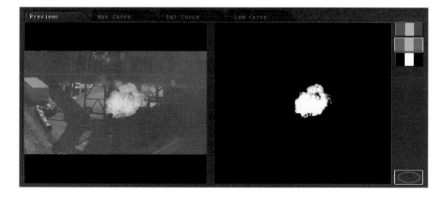

The yellow orange color of the flame is selected as a key.

**4**   Adjust the HSL qualifiers as needed, and increase the key blur parameter to about .3 to soften the edge of the key.

**5**   Press Control-9 to add a keyframe for the current room.

**6**   Press the Right Arrow key to move about two-thirds of the way through the clip.

**NOTE ▶** You may wish to adjust the track heights in the Timeline to see the Secondaries keyframe track better.

**7** Press Control-9 to add a second keyframe.

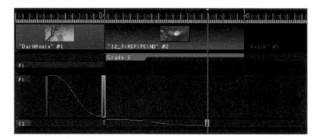

**8** Set the Matte Preview Control to Final (red-green-blue).

**9** Set the Control pop-up menu to Outside, so that your adjustments affect the area outside of the flame.

**10** Lower the Saturation control to 0.

Because you set the two keyframes, Color will automate the transformation, slowly draining out the color (except for the flame) over the course of the shot.

**11** Play the clip.

**12** To speed up the change, drag the keyframes closer together in the Timeline. To slow it down, drag them farther apart.

> **TIP** ▶ Each Secondary room has its own set of keyframes that will appear on its own track in the Timeline.

## Changing Interpolation Settings

Whenever you create multiple keyframes, Color must calculate the proper settings for the frames between them. This is called *interpolation*. You can control the way Color interpolates your settings by choosing one of three modes:

**Smooth**—The parameters begin and end changing slowly, creating an organic easing effect that helps to hide the precise locations of the keyframes. This is the default interpolation method.

**Linear**—The parameters make a steady, uniform progression from the starting value to the ending value. This can be useful when an effect begins and ends on the first and last frames of a clip, but otherwise it may draw attention to the keyframe positions by causing a sudden value change.

**Constant**—The value from the previous keyframe is applied to all interim frames. Effectively this setting disables interpolation, allowing you to create an effect in which a value changes suddenly on a precise frame.

The interpolation method can be changed for the range between any two keyframes. For example, you can create an effect where the values stay constant between the first two keyframes, then move smoothly to the third, and so on. To change the interpolation method, you must park on the left keyframe, then toggle through the three methods.

**1** Play the clip and observe the way the desaturation effect occurs.

**2** Press Option-Left Arrow or Option-Right Arrow to move the playhead to the left keyframe.

**3** Choose Timeline > Change Keyframe or press Control-8.

The interpolation switches from Smooth to Linear.

**4** Play the clip.

In this instance the difference between smooth and linear is somewhat subtle, but it is observable, especially when watching the scopes.

**5** Repeat steps 2 and 3.

The interpolation switches to Constant.

**6** Play the clip.

Now the values don't change at all until the second keyframe is reached, creating a very different effect, and not one you would likely use in this case.

**7** Repeat steps 2 and 3 again to return the interpolation to Smooth.

## Animating User Shapes

One of the most powerful uses for keyframing in Color is in modifying the shape and position of a mask over time to accommodate movement in the frame.

**1** In the Timeline, press the Down Arrow key to move to the next clip.

**2**   Play the clip.

This clip shows a group of people running along the beach. There is some camera movement to keep the people centered in the frame.

Creating a vignette around the ocean would allow you to enhance the color of the water; however, because of the camera movement, the vignette would have to be animated to stay aligned with the image. This is a perfect time to employ keyframing.

**3**   Press Command-3 to open the Secondaries room (if it's not already open).

**4**   Select the Enable checkbox to turn on Secondary 1.

For the sake of simplifying the lesson, some settings have already been applied to both the Inside and Outside for this secondary. Color is just waiting for you to draw a shape around the ocean.

**5**   Select the Vignette checkbox, and from the Shape pop-up menu, choose User Shape.

The Geometry room is automatically opened.

**6**   Create a shape that outlines the ocean. You can use the picture below as a guide.

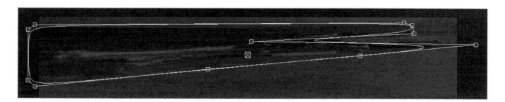

**TIP** ▶ To zoom in and out on the Geometry room preview area, right-click and drag left or right.

**NOTE** ▶ In the real world, you would likely soften the edges of such a shape, but for the sake of the keyframing lesson, leave the mask with a hard edge. This makes it much easier to see how effective your keyframing is, and you can always add the softness later.

**7**   Click Attach.

This connects the shape to the secondary and enables it for keyframing.

**8**   Making sure you're parked on frame 1, press Control-9 to add your first keyframe.

**9**   In the Timeline, press End to move to the last frame of the clip.

Drag handle

**10**  Press Control-9 to add a second keyframe.

**11**  Drag the green box at the center of the shape (called the *drag handle*) to realign the shape with the new position of the ocean. You'll also need to adjust some of the control points on the upper-right corner of the shape to account for the new camera position.

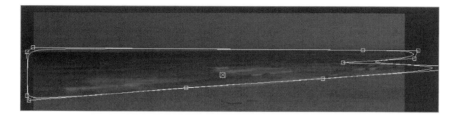

**12** In the Timeline, step through the clip, frame by frame, and watch the shape position.

## Adding Intermediary Keyframes

Although the beginning and end of the shot now look correct, unfortunately the camera move doesn't line up very well with the automatic interpolation between the first and last frames. This effect is going to require more than two keyframes.

There is no limit to the number of keyframes you can create (other than the number of frames in your clip); however, in most cases the fewer keyframes you use, the smoother your effect. This shot obviously requires some additional keyframes, but for optimal results, you should try to determine the best places to put them so that you can create as few as possible.

**1**   Use the arrow keys to step through the shot frame by frame.

About midway through the shot (at approximately 17:00), the camera tilt levels off momentarily and the mask position is misaligned.

2   Press Control-9 to add a new keyframe at that point, and drag the shape to realign it with the ocean.

Adding a new keyframe automatically forces new interpolation between the first keyframe and this one, and between this one and the ending frame.

3   Step through the entire clip again.

Now, the first half seems pretty well aligned, but the second half still seems a bit disconnected.

4   Move the playhead approximately halfway between the second set of keyframes, and press Control-9 to add a new keyframe at that point.

5   Adjust the shape's position (and its control points, if necessary) to align it with the ocean on the current frame.

6   Once again, step through the entire clip.

Repeat these steps as needed until the mask accurately follows the camera move.

This method works well for simple movement such as the example above. For more complex movement, you can employ Color's motion tracking tool (covered in Lesson 9).

## Keyframing Color Effects

Just like these other rooms, Color FX can be keyframed, and as in the other rooms you only get one keyframe track, regardless of how many nodes are applied, or how many parameters each node contains. However, each individual node can be keyframed independently.

When a node is selected, the Color FX keyframe track displays only keyframes for that one node. Selecting a different node replaces the contents of the keyframe track with its own keyframes. Understanding this will help prevent you from panicking when you see keyframes appearing and disappearing while you work in the Color FX room.

Adding keyframing skills to your mastery of the myriad grading tools in each of Color's rooms takes you beyond the beginner stage and prepares you to tackle many of the real-world challenges that colorists face on a daily basis.

## Lesson Review

1. Which rooms can be keyframed?
2. Can individual parameters be keyframed?
3. What are keyframes for?
4. How are keyframes added?
5. Do you set the value before adding a keyframe or add a keyframe before setting values?
6. How do you delete an individual keyframe?
7. Name and describe each of Color's interpolation modes.
8. How do you make a shape keyframable?
9. How many keyframes can be added to a clip?
10. Can Color FX nodes be keyframed individually?

### Answers

1. All rooms can be keyframed.
2. No.
3. Keyframes allow you to animate effects over time.
4. By choosing Timeline > Add Keyframe or pressing Control-9.
5. Always add a keyframe first.
6. Park on that keyframe and choose Timeline > Remove Keyframe.

7.  Smooth: Creates gradual organic transitions between keyframes.
    Linear: Creates uniform progression between keyframes.
    Constant: Holds the value of the previous keyframe.

8.  It must be attached to a secondary correction.

9.  One per frame.

10. Yes.

# 9

**Lesson Files**   Color Book Files > Lesson Files > Lesson 09 > Geometry.colorproj

**Time**   This lesson takes approximately 75 minutes to complete.

**Goals**   Recompose shots to correct framing errors or redefine the focus of a shot

Animate pan and scan effects to add simulated camera movement or accommodate a smaller screen size than the source footage

Track motion within the frame

Attach trackers to vignettes to animate secondary corrections

Manually track objects that can't be automatically tracked

Control tracking smoothness to finesse an animation path

# Recomposing and Tracking

Although Color is primarily a color-correction tool, for many projects it falls in the category of "finishing" software. Color's output is often the last stop before exhibition, so it offers a few critical features in the Geometry room to perform last-minute motion effects such as reframing a shot, and it has full-fledged pan-and-scan tools. This can be essential if you're preparing a show for an output method other than the acquisition format, such as outputting a 4:3 version of a 16:9 show, or an SD version of an HD show, and so on.

The Geometry room is also where you perform motion tracking for shots where a mask or correction needs to move around the frame to follow a particular object. Color's tracking mechanism is simplistic, which makes it easy to employ, and its usefulness is limited to straightforward tracking applications. Remember, Color is not a full-fledged compositing tool, and for nearly all color-correction tasks, its tracker is perfectly adequate. If you have a shot requiring three-dimensional or multipoint tracking, try Motion or Shake.

## Using the Geometry Room

The Geometry room is where you perform any physical manipulation to your shots, such as panning and scanning, creating user shapes (which you've done in several previous lessons), and tracking object movement within the frame.

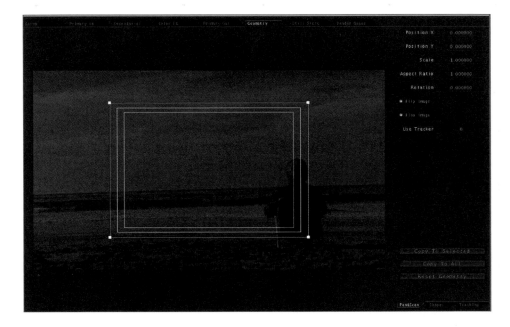

The large preview area gives ample space for performing these manipulations and changes dynamically depending on the active mode. The three tabs on the right (Pan&Scan, Shapes, and Tracking) control which mode is active and contain the different settings each mode requires.

You can almost think of these as three different rooms. In fact, Pan&Scan and Shapes each have their own keyframe tracks. (Tracking is a sort of keyframing operation and so does not require a keyframe track in the Timeline.)

## Recomposing Shots

The Pan&Scan tab facilitates zooming in and out and rotating and manipulating your clips in space, much like Final Cut Pro's Motion tab. You can perform a single, static operation, such as enlarging a two-shot to turn it into a single, or you can perform dynamic effects using keyframes such as adding a zoom during a shot.

**1**   Open Lesson Files > Lesson 09 > **Geometry.colorproj**.

**2**   Choose File > Reconnect Media and navigate to Lesson Files > Lesson 09 > Media, then click Choose.

**3**   Press Command-6 to open the Geometry room.

**4**   Click the Pan&Scan tab if it isn't already open.

Although this room allows you to manipulate clips with results similar to what you get using motion effects in Final Cut Pro, the interface works in almost the opposite way. Be aware that moving from one software package to the other requires a bit of a mental readjustment.

For example, in Final Cut Pro, you drag clips and position them in a static Canvas. To zoom in on a clip, you enlarge the clip so that it appears bigger in the frame.

In Color's Geometry room, the clip never changes size or position. Instead, you adjust the size and position of the *frame*. To zoom in on a clip, you shrink the frame so that it displays only a limited portion of the original image.

**TIP** ▸ The red outer frame indicates the actual frame boundary. The two inner white frames indicate action-safe and title-safe boundaries to aid in your framing decisions.

Although Final Cut Pro users might find that this takes a little getting used to, it's very intuitive in its own right. Plus, you always have the Viewer right there to show you what your final frame is going to look like.

**TIP** ▸ The settings in Final Cut Pro's Motion tab and Color's Pan&Scan tab are actually linked together: If you send a clip to Color containing Motion settings, the Geometry room will automatically display those same settings, and if you send a clip from Color back to FCP, any Pan & Scan work will be translated to Motion settings.

The size of the frame is determined by the Resolution setting in the Project Settings tab of the Setup room.

5   Press Command-1 to open the Setup room.

6   Click the Project Settings tab.

7   Examine the Resolution Presets.

This project is set to 720 x 486 NTSC SD, although the source footage is all HD.

8   Press Command-6 to return to the Geometry room.

The HD footage used in this lesson is larger than these new project settings, so the frame boundaries in the Geometry room appear smaller than the source clip. While the Geometry room preview shows the whole clip, the Viewer shows the output as determined by the size and position of the frame.

9   Click anywhere inside the frame boundary, and drag to reposition it and change the portion of the source clip that is displayed in the Viewer.

**10** Drag the frame so that the man is nicely framed in the right third of the screen.

You can also grow or shrink the frame to zoom in or out on the image, or rotate the frame to rotate the image (in the opposite direction).

**11** Drag any corner of the frame and enlarge it as far as you can without exceeding the edges of the source video.

This image also has a slight clockwise tilt to it.

**12** Drag any edge of the frame to rotate it counterclockwise to make the horizon appear level in the Viewer.

**TIP** ▶ Be sure to watch the image in the Viewer and not in the Geometry room to see when the horizon looks level.

You may have to shrink the frame slightly to ensure that there is no black edge visible in the corners of the frame, which would reveal the artificial frame manipulations you've created.

**TIP** ▶ Zooming in on an image (by shrinking the frame beyond its default size) will soften the image and may reveal image noise, blockiness, or other artifacts. The size and compression format of the source image, and the amount of enlargement you perform, determine the degree of these undesirable effects.

## Animating Pan and Scan Effects

In addition to simply reframing shots, you can use keyframes to create a wide variety of motion effects in the Geometry room, from subtle corrections to radical new camera movement.

**1** In the Timeline, press the Down Arrow key to move to the next shot.

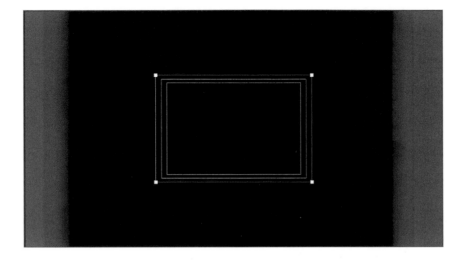

**2**  Drag the playhead through the Timeline to view the whole clip while watching the Geometry preview area.

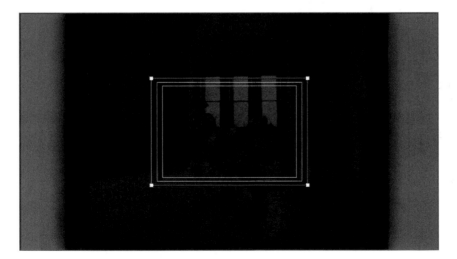

This show was transferred from film (telecined) at full frame, specifically to allow for reframing in post. It was also captured at a full 1920 x 1080 frame size, so it can be safely resized, even in a 1280 x 720 project. The white bars on the left and right of the image are artifacts from the telecine process and are not intended to be seen in any situation.

The source footage contains a horizontal dolly move, revealing the chandelier through the doorway as the camera passes by. In this example, you'll add another movement, offsetting the dolly move somewhat (to keep the chandelier in frame as long as possible) and creating a vertical "boom" movement to emphasize the fact that the chandelier is on the floor, where it's not supposed to be.

**3**   Press the Up Arrow key to move the playhead to the first frame of the clip.

**4**   Press Control-9 to add a keyframe.

**5**   Position the frame in the Geometry preview area at the upper-right corner of the visible part of the frame.

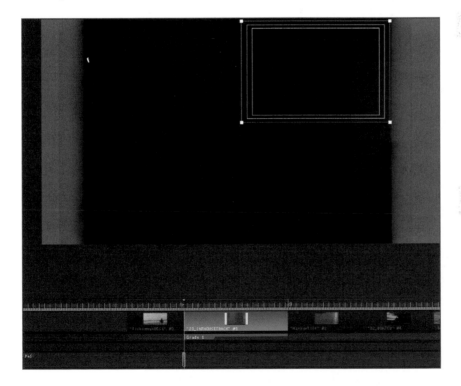

**6**   Press the Down Arrow key, then the Left Arrow key once to move to the last frame of the clip.

**7**   Press Control-9 to add a second keyframe.

**8** Drag the frame to the lower-left corner of the visible area in the Geometry preview area.

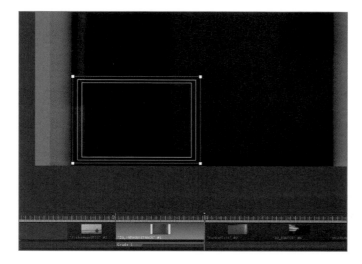

**9** Play the clip.

The overall effect is good, but if you stop halfway through, you can see that the chandelier is not quite fully visible in the frame.

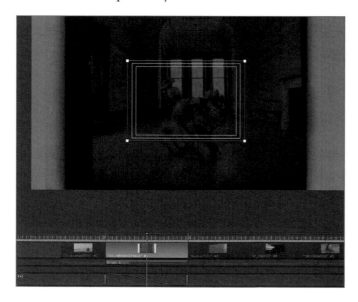

By adding a third keyframe midway through, you can improve the overall move.

**10**  Position the playhead midway through the clip, and press Control-9 to add a keyframe.

**11**  Position the frame to contain more of the chandelier.

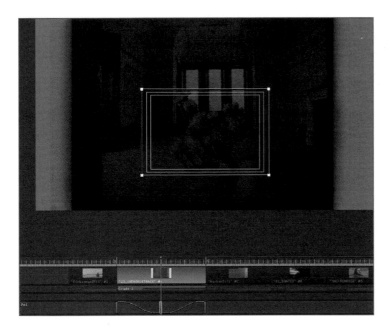

**12**  Play the clip.

While this solved one problem, it created another. Now the camera move appears to stall midway through the shot, undermining the momentum of the original material. This is because of Color's default keyframe interpolation, which adds an "ease in/ease out" effect at each keyframe.

In this case, changing the interpolation to Linear will give a more desirable effect. Interpolation can be set only on the leftmost keyframe for each section.

**13**  Press Option-Left Arrow to move the playhead to the first keyframe.

**14**  Choose Timeline > Change Keyframe (or press Control-8) to set the interpolation to Linear.

**15**  Press Option-Right Arrow to move to the middle keyframe.

**16**  Press Control-8 to change this keyframe to Linear as well.

**17**  Play the clip.

Now the animated pan and scan effect doesn't pause midway through the shot.

This shot can be recomposed in a wide variety of ways. Experiment on your own with different ways of displaying the shot. Remember that you can zoom in and out, rotate the image, and use the different interpolation settings to create linear, smooth, or constant (which will pause the movement between two keyframes) motion effects.

## Tracking Objects

Moving shots always provide additional challenges for colorists, especially when using secondaries that operate on specific objects within the frame. When an object can be isolated based on a specific color, you can use keyframes to follow any movement within the shot. When keys won't work, you can employ Color's tracking tool to follow objects that move in the frame.

**1**  Press the Down Arrow key to move to the next shot and play it.

This shot already has some primary corrections to improve the overall contrast, but it could be greatly improved by adding a vignette to give some more sunset color and blue to the sky.

2   Press Command-3 to open the Secondaries room.

3   Move the playhead midway through the clip so that the buildings are visible in the frame.

4   Enable Secondary #1, and select the Vignette checkbox.

5   Set the Vignette shape to Square. In the preview area, enlarge, position, and soften the mask to cover the top half of the frame as pictured below.

**6**  Set the Matte Preview control to Final.

**7**  With the Control pop-up menu set to Inside, lower the Shadow contrast slider to bring out more detail in the buildings (until the blacks on the left of the frame hit 0% in the Waveform Monitor), and move the Midtone color balance control toward orange to add more saturation to the masked area.

**8**  Set the Control pop-up menu to Outside, and move the Shadow, Midtone, and Highlight color balance controls toward blue to add a touch more color to the water.

**9**  Play the clip.

Oops! The correction sure looked good on that one frame, but it needs to follow the camera move to be useful in this shot. Enter the tracker.

**10** Press Command-6 to open the Geometry room, and click the Tracking tab to access the motion tracker controls.

**11** Make sure the playhead is on the first frame of the clip, and click the New button.

A new tracker is added and appears in the list at the top of the tab. (You can have many trackers applied to each clip.)

The inner box of the tracker identifies the specific object in the image you want Color to track, and the outer box provides the range where Color will search for that object in the subsequent frames. You can move and resize both boxes directly in the preview area. If the object's movement is fast, you will likely need a larger search box.

Tracking is most effective on high-contrast areas and video noise reduces its efficacy, so you must choose your tracking location carefully. In this image, there's not very much to choose from at all.

**12** Reposition and resize the tracker so that the tip of the island is in the inner box and the outer box surrounds it with a small search area.

**TIP** ▸ If the outer (search) box is too small and the tracked object moves too far, too fast, the tracker may not be able to find it, and your tracking operation will fail. On the other hand, if the search box is too large, it might intersect another similar object in the frame, and the tracker might start following the wrong object.

**13** Click the Process button.

Color steps through the clip frame by frame and tracks the object. A progress bar is displayed in the Tracker tab, and as the growing green bar in the Tracker area of the Timeline.

**NOTE** ▸ Although in this example, you track the entire clip from the first to last frame, Trackers can have In and Out points to limit their action to a subsection of a clip.

## Applying Tracking Data to Corrections

Of course, just tracking the object doesn't have any effect on the image. In order to use that information, you must attach it to a correction. In this case, you'll attach it to the secondary vignette you created earlier.

**1**   Press Command-3 to open the Secondaries room.

**2**   In the Vignette section, type *1* in the Use Tracker field if it's not already there.

> **TIP** ▶ To disconnect a tracker from the vignette, enter *0* in the Use Tracker field.

The vignette position is linked to the tracker data.

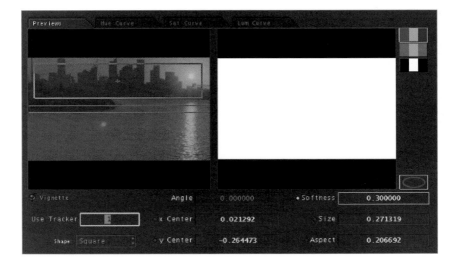

**3**   Play the clip.

The effect now moves along with the camera move.

## Offsetting the Vignette

This is a deceptively easy example because the object you tracked is in nearly the exact same position as the center of the vignette. Often this won't be the case. You can track any high-contrast object in the image and manually offset the position of the vignette to affect a different part of the image.

In this case, the vignette can be offset slightly to better align it with the horizon.

> **NOTE ▶** In actuality, this example would benefit from replacing the square shape with a custom-drawn shape that could include the bluff on the left side of the frame. Because this is a lesson on tracking and not on masks, the simple square is used to reduce the overall number of steps.

**1**    In the Secondaries preview area, drag the mask to a new position so that the yellow line (indicating the center of the soft edge) lines up more closely with the horizon.

**2**    Play the clip.

The vignette still moves along with the tracker data, but it's offset by the amount you dragged. You can do this on any frame in the clip, and the offset will automatically be calculated forward and backward. Just note that every time you move the vignette, you're resetting the offset value.

## Manual Tracking

In many instances, tracking can't be done automatically. Something else in the frame obscures the tracked object, or the object moves off the edge of the screen, or sometimes there just isn't an object with high enough contrast to track at all.

**1**    Press the Down Arrow key to move to the next clip.

**2** Play the clip.

This clip presents a very challenging tracking case. If you wanted to change the color of the boat, or add a tint to the windshield, or do any number of other corrections that would rely on following the boat's movement in the frame, you would first need to track that movement. However, any of the obvious points for tracking become obscured by splashing water or by the boat moving off the edge of the frame. This means automatic tracking won't work.

Fortunately, Color has a well-implemented "manual" tracking mechanism. In the next exercise, you'll track the boat's movement.

Before you begin tracking, think about what object in the frame will be a good target. Look for any spot that will be easy to recognize, and that remains visible throughout the duration of the clip.

For this clip, the right edge of the dark blue line on the boat's hull is a pretty good target. It stays mostly above the water and is a clear enough edge that it should be relatively easy to keep track of (literally).

**3** Position the playhead on the first frame of the clip.

**4** In the Tracking tab of the Geometry room, click New.

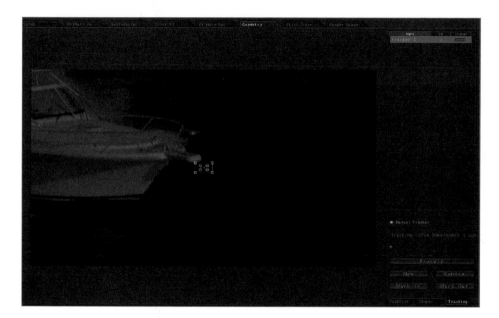

A new tracker is added to the preview area.

5   Select the Manual Tracker checkbox.

The tracker becomes a single green square, which indicates that Color is awaiting your input for where the tracker should begin.

The next time you click, you'll define the starting position of the tracker, so don't click carelessly! Do not click the green box or attempt to drag it to the starting position.

6   Click the right edge of the dark blue line on the boat's hull.

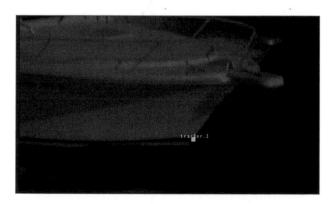

When you make that click, several things happen. The green point turns red and is recorded as the tracker's position for that frame. Then, Color automatically advances the video by one frame and awaits your next click.

At first this can be confusing, but it actually makes the manual tracking procedure easy.

**7** Click the new position of the right edge of the dark blue line.

Again, the clip is advanced one frame.

**8** Continue clicking the blue line, frame after frame.

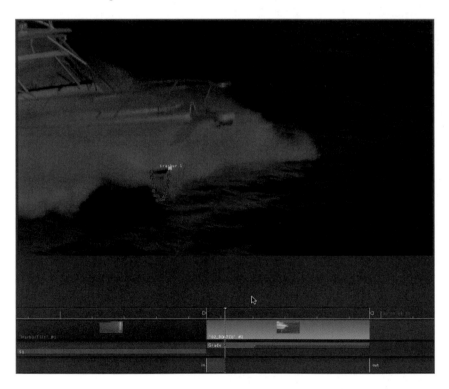

**NOTE ▶** There are some frames where it will be difficult to see the exact position of the target. First of all, you can zoom in on the preview area by right-clicking (Control-clicking) and dragging left or right, and if you still can't see it, guess. Don't worry about getting everything perfect. You can always go back and clean up an errant frame position if necessary.

**TIP** ▶ If you have a few individual tracking points that appear to be out of place, you can fix them by moving the playhead to that particular frame and clicking a new position (not dragging the point) in the tracking preview area.

Once you've reached the last frame, *Tracker 1* will appear in green text. Then you can smooth the overall motion path.

9   Drag the Tracking Curve Smoothness slider.

If you go too far, the tracker may no longer follow your target precisely, but a small bit of smoothing can greatly improve the overall effect of the tracker.

Now it's up to you to come up with a vignette to attach to this tracker. Perhaps you want to tint the windshield of the boat, or even apply a user-drawn shape to turn the white deck blue. Whatever you choose to do, you won't be able to judge its effectiveness until you attempt to use the tracker to perform an effect. And beware, this is an extremely difficult shot. You may need to add keyframes to the vignette shape to achieve your desired effect.

**NOTE ▶** Do not deselect the Manual Tracker checkbox; doing so will delete all of your tracking marks.

Finally, for extra credit, there is one more shot in the project: the swimming woman.

Add a tracker to her lips or nostrils (or any other high-contrast area), and create a tracked vignette to turn her face bluish (to suggest that the water is cold).

Although many projects never need such tools, mastering these effects in the Geometry room broadens your capabilities as a colorist and expands the types of projects and clients you'll be ready to take on. As you get more comfortable with these effects, you'll undoubtedly find many new and unexpected uses for them, beyond even their intended purpose.

## Lesson Review

1.  What does the red outline in the Pan & Scan preview area represent?

2.  When zooming in on a shot, should the red outline get bigger or smaller?

3.  How can pan and scan effects be changed over time?

4.  What does a Constant keyframe interpolation do to a Pan & Scan move?

5.  Describe an ideal tracking target.

6.  What will make automatic tracking impossible?

7.  How does adding a tracker change the image?

8.  How is manual tracking done?

9.  Can manual tracking points be corrected after they're created?

10. How can a track be smoothed once it has been created?

*Answers*

1.  The frame boundary.

2.  Smaller.

3.  Using keyframes.

4.  It freezes the movement for the duration between the two keyframes.

5.  A small high-contrast object that is visible for the duration of the shot.

6.  If the target becomes obscured or moves beyond the frame boundary.

7.  Adding a tracker by itself has no effect on the image.

8.  By clicking once per frame on a target object, which automatically creates a path.

9.  Yes, by positioning the playhead on a particular frame and clicking to create a new tracking point.

10. By using the Tracking Curve Smoothness slider in the Tracking tab of the Geometry room.

# 10

## Lesson Files

## Time

This lesson takes approximately 60 minutes to complete.

## Goals

Make final adjustments to a project using the Primary Out room

Create a stylized look using Primary Out

Use groups to apply stylized Primary Out corrections

Making a project broadcast safe

Add files to the Render Queue

Render files and import into Final Cut Pro

Save and load archived projects

# Lesson **10**

# Primary Out and Rendering

The last step to finishing a project in Color is to add any final tweaks or effects using the Primary Out room, and then to render the project and send it back to Final Cut Pro. You may also want to manually adjust the program to keep it broadcast safe rather than using the Broadcast Safe checkbox in the Setup room. Another option when you finish a project is to export it for use in a different editing application.

The Primary Out room uses the output of the previous rooms—Primary In, Secondaries, and Color FX—and creates the final, composited image. One of the biggest advantages of using the Primary Out room for final tweaks and looks is that you can grade a program to a neutral, balanced look, and then apply subtle changes to all the shots in the program without affecting any of the primary or secondary corrections. If you decide to manually correct your project to bring it into broadcast-safe specifications using the Primary Out room, you can avoid the clipping that the Setup room's Broadcast Safe setting often imposes.

## Global Changes and Final Tweaks

Visually and functionally, the Primary Out room is nearly identical to the Primary In room. You can make the same kinds of changes in both rooms. Although there are many strategies to grading a project, a common workflow is to use the Primary Out room to make subtle changes to the project's global look. This allows the colorist to keep the basic color corrections for each individual clip unchanged while making global tweaks to the look of the project.

**1**   Open Lesson Files > Lesson 10 > **A_FinalProject_Start.colorproj**.

**2**   Choose File > Reconnect Media and navigate to Lesson Files > Lesson 10 > Media, then click Choose.

**3**   Click the Primary Out tab or press Command-5 to open the Primary Out room.

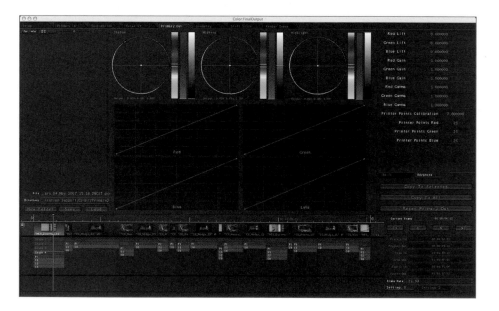

This project is similar to the project you worked on in Lesson 5. You'll start by making some subtle adjustments to one of the shots, and then you'll apply those adjustments to the rest of the project. For this session, you'll use the Broadcast Safe setting in the Setup room to handle bringing the whites and blacks into the broadcast-safe range. Later in this lesson, you'll make those adjustments manually.

**4**  Click the Setup tab or press Command-1 to open the Setup room.

**5**  At the bottom of the Setup room, click the Project Settings tab.

**6**  Verify that the Broadcast Safe checkbox at the top of the Project Settings tab is selected.

**7**  As mentioned in Lesson 1, this setting simply clips values that exceed the legal limit. Later, you'll manually adjust the image to bring it into broadcast-safe range.

**8**  Press Command-5 to open the Primary Out room.

**9**  Double-click shot 4 in the sequence (**CU_Henry_04**) to make it the active clip.

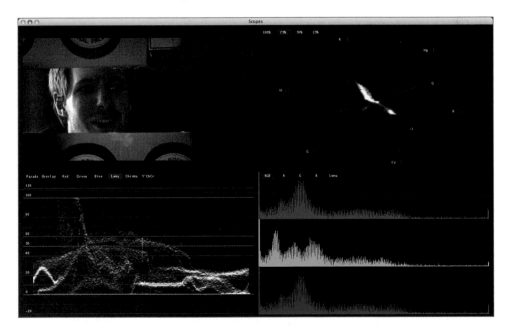

You'll use this image as the basis for your final tweaks to this project. The clients have decided that they'd like a little less contrast and saturation.

**10**  Using the Highlight contrast slider, bring the highlights down until they register around 95% in the Waveform Monitor.

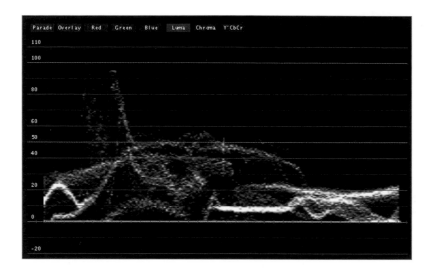

If you look at shot 4 in the Timeline, it will now have an additional correction under it, labeled *PO*. (If you don't see it, move the playhead to another shot and then back to the fourth shot.)

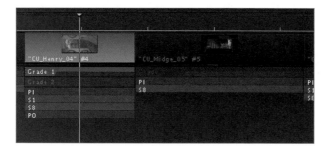

**11** Using the Basic tab of the Primary Out room, change the Shadow Sat. setting to .5—reducing the saturation of the darker areas only.

These changes are quite subtle, but they've toned down the intensity of the overall look. Now we need to apply these settings to the rest of the shots in the project.

**12** Click the Copy To All button just under the Basic and Advanced tabs of the Primary Out room.

Just as in the Primary In room, the Copy To All button copies the correction that has been applied to the current shot to all the shots in the project. In this case, the highlight contrast and shadow saturation corrections are copied to every shot in the project. Each shot should now have a Primary Out correction visible in the Timeline.

## Modifying and Replacing Primary Out Room Settings

After reviewing the newly adjusted project, the clients have decided on some additional changes. Using a different shot, you'll adjust the Primary Out correction and then apply that to all the shots in the project. The corrections you need to make involve reducing the overall saturation and brightening up the midtones of the project.

**1** Double-click the first clip in the Timeline (shot 1, **MCU_Doorway_01**) to select it.

> **NOTE ►** Remember that if you want to scrub a value in Color, you place the pointer over the numeric entry field, press and hold the middle mouse button, and scrub left to right.

**2**   Using the Master Gamma setting of the Basic tab in the Primary Out room, raise the gamma setting to brighten the shot. (A value of 1.1 works well for this example.)

**3**   Using the Saturation setting of the Basic tab in the Primary Out room, lower the overall saturation to about .85.

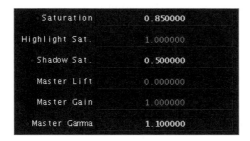

**4**   Click the Copy To All button just under the Basic and Advanced tabs of the Primary Out room.

As before, this step applies the Primary Out changes made to the selected clip to all the clips in the project, replacing any prior Primary Out settings.

**5**   Play the Timeline to see how the new settings look.

**NOTE** ▶ Timeline playback mode should already be set to movie mode. If only a single clip plays, press Shift-Command-M to toggle playback mode to movie mode from clip mode.

If you'd like to review your changes, shot 1 (the first clip in the Timeline—**MCU_Doorway_01**) has the original settings saved in grade 3. To do a before-and-after comparison, simply alternate between grade 3 and grade 4 by clicking each grade while the clip is visible in the preview area, or use Control-3 and Control-4 to select each grade.

**NOTE** ▶ As with the Primary In room, if you want to reset all of the Primary Out changes, click the Reset Primary Out button at the lower-right corner of the Primary Out room. If you want to reset the Primary Out settings for all the clips in the project, click the Reset Primary Out button followed by the Copy To All button.

## Creating a Stylized Look for a Finished Project

Now that you've used Color to make subtle changes to a finished project, you'll make a more stylized change, which again will be applied to all of the shots in the project. As with subtle changes, using the Primary Out room to create a stylized look allows you to make your initial corrections to a neutral color balance and then experiment from there using the Primary Out room. Because Primary Out room stylized effects are separate from the other color corrections, they can be easily modified or removed without changing the initial work done to bring all the shots to a uniform neutral look.

Keep in mind that the following exercise is to create a stylized look requested by the clients that departs from your base corrections. You want to be able to make the changes without affecting your initial corrections. Whether or not you like the end result is something for you and the clients to discuss!

1    Open Lesson Files > Lesson 10 > **B_FinalProject_Stylized.colorproj**.

2    Choose File > Reconnect Media and navigate to Lesson Files > Lesson 10 > Media, then click Choose.

3    If the Waveform Monitor is not displayed in the Viewer window, right-click (Control-click) a displayed scope, and choose Waveform. Click the Luma button if the waveform is not already set to Luma mode.

4    Click the Primary Out tab or press Command-5 to open the Primary Out Room.

5    Double-click the first clip in the Timeline (shot 1) to select it. Make sure grade 4 is selected.

6    Drag the Shadow color balance control toward blue to cool off the darker parts of the image.

7    Drag the Highlight color balance control toward yellow to add warmth back to the bricks.

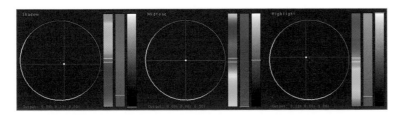

Next, you'll flatten the highlights considerably so that the exterior shots don't over-whelm the much-darker interior shots.

**8** Pull the white handle (right side) of the Luma curve downward until the highlights fall below 80% on the Waveform Monitor.

**9** Click the Luma curve to add another handle near the fourth vertical line in the background grid, and drag upward to brighten up the midtones. Drag upward until the curve crosses the midpoint of both the third horizontal and third vertical line in the background grid.

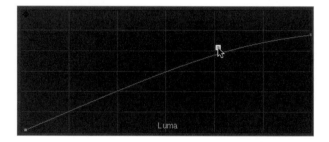

By adding the second handle, you've restored the lower portion of the curve to its original shape, which leaves the darker portions of the image unchanged.

The next three shots in the project have already had Primary Out corrections applied to create a look similar to the one you just added to the first shots.

Now you'll apply those Primary Out corrections to the rest of the shots using the groups created in Lesson 5.

## Applying Stylized Primary Out Corrections to Grouped Clips

In Lesson 5, you created and used groups as a way to apply a grade to similar shots. Now you'll use those same groups to apply a Primary Out correction to similar shots. The groups consist of shots that are similar to each other and can be corrected using the same grade. For example, all of the doorway clips that need to be corrected are in group 3, so you'll use shot 1 to correct that group.

**1** Press Command-1 to open the Setup room.

**2**   Click the Shots tab to open the Shots browser.

**3**   If icon view is not already displayed, click the Icon View button.

> **NOTE ▶** Remember that you can zoom in and out in the Shots browser while in icon view by dragging the right mouse button left or right. To scroll the window, hold the middle mouse button while moving the mouse.

**4**   If necessary, scroll so that Group 3 is visible.

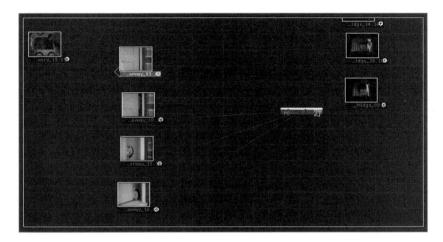

**5**   Drag the Primary Out correction from shot 1 onto the Group 3 icon. If you don't see your PO correction, move the playhead to another shot and then back to shot 1.

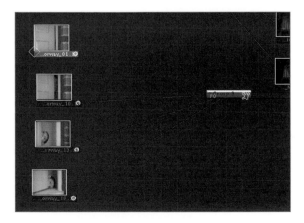

**NOTE ►** Make sure you drag the Primary Out correction only, not the entire grade. You want to add the Primary Out correction to whatever grade is already applied to the clips in Group 3.

The Doorway clips now have a Primary Out stylized correction applied to them.

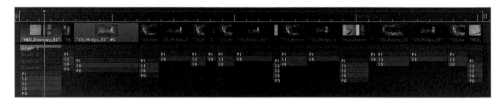

6 Scroll in the Shots browser until Group 1 and Group 2 are visible.

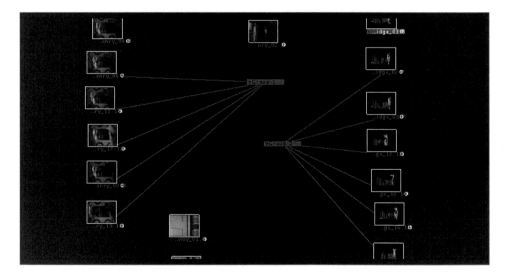

7 Drag the Primary Out correction from shot 3 onto the Group 2 icon.

8 Drag the Primary Out correction from shot 4 onto the Group 1 icon.

You have now applied a stylized look to your project without affecting the initial grading that you did to create the initial look of the project. You can easily remove all of the stylized Primary Out corrections using the technique mentioned earlier in this lesson.

## Manually Controlling Broadcast-Safe Output

As mentioned in Lesson 1, video for broadcast needs to conform to certain standards to be legal. Although a complete discussion of broadcast-safe standards is beyond the scope of this book, let's quickly review the basics.

Typically, an NTSC video signal for broadcast must not have digital luma black values below 0 or luma white values above 100. The chroma portion of the signal also needs to stay within legal limits, although the definition of legal chroma is somewhat harder to discern. The legal value of chroma varies based on the luma value, but in its most conservative definition, it falls within the color bar target graticules on the Vectorscope.

Additionally, different broadcasters may have specific guidelines that you need to follow when you submit program material for broadcast. It's always best to check to see if you have specific targets you have to meet for a particular broadcaster.

> **TIP** When delivering a product for broadcast over cable or TV networks, always consult with the distributor first and request a delivery tech spec sheet. Given that many programs ultimately are repurposed and delivered over many different media, it's imperative to ensure that the quality is maintained by staying within the specs.

You can also monitor your signal using external scopes if your hardware setup allows it. You would still make corrections in Color as you would using its internal software-based scopes, but you would base your corrections on the feedback provided by the hardware scopes.

> **TIP** Tectronix, Omnitek, Videotek, and Leader, among others, make very high-quality vectroscope/waveform equipment that is ideal for external monitoring in addition to Color's internal scopes.

Many video recording devices allowing recording of a signal that does not meet broadcast standards, and applying corrections and FX to shots also can also push the signal beyond the bounds of legality.

Although the Broadcast Safe checkbox in the Project Settings tab of the Setup room provides a quick and easy way to ensure that your video is broadcast legal, it does so by clipping the signal. Areas of the signal that are more than 5 percent above legal white are simply clipped to legal white. This technique can result in areas of blown-out highlights, where no detail is visible.

If you have source material that has important detail in the shadows and highlights, you can retain more of that detail by manually controlling how the image is made broadcast safe. Using the Primary Out room, you can make a shot broadcast safe while preserving important detail in the shot that would otherwise be lost. However, you are responsible for careful monitoring of every shot (and really, every frame) to make sure the resulting program falls within broadcast-safe limits.

> **TIP** ▶ Many cameras can shoot from 0% (black) to 110%–120% (white). White values above 100% are known as super-white and are not broadcast legal. The Broadcast Safe feature can be very harsh when dealing with these clips. It's often best to manually adjust the clips to around 98%–100% white, and then clip (using Broadcast Safe) that value as a safety net.

The first step is to open up your project and deselect Broadcast Safe.

**1** Open Lesson Files > Lesson 10 > **C_FinalProject_Broadcast.colorproj.**

**2** Choose File > Reconnect Media and navigate to Lesson Files > Lesson 10 > Media, then click Choose.

**3** Press Command-1 to open the Setup room.

**4** Click the Project Settings tab.

**5** Deselect Broadcast Safe at the top of the Project Settings tab.

**6** If the Waveform Monitor is not visible, right-click a visible scope and choose Waveform. Click the Luma button above the Waveform Monitor.

**7** If the Vectorscope is not visible, right-click a visible scope (other than the Waveform) and choose Vectorscope. Click the 75% button above the Vectorscope.

**8** Toggle playback mode to Clip if necessary using Command-Shift-M.

**9** Click the User Prefs tab.

**10** Make sure Update UI During Playback is active. If you're using one display, make sure Update Primary Display is active. If you're using two displays, activate both Update Primary Display and Update Secondary Display.

Activating Update UI During Playback allows you to see the scopes while playing back a clip. It also shows you how a grade changes the various settings and how they change if you created keyframes.

For this exercise, watching the Waveform Monitor during playback allows you to check the entire shot for broadcast legality without having to step through it frame by frame.

**TIP** ▶ Keep in mind that a single frame may have values that exceed broadcast-safe values. If you notice transient glints or sparkles, it may be best to step through those frames to check for legality, or use the Broadcast Safe feature.

**11** Double-click the first shot to select it.

**12** Play the shot and watch the Waveform Monitor.

## Adjusting Black Levels

The white levels for this shot appear to be legal—they stay well below the 100% line near the top of the Waveform Monitor. However, the black levels fall well below legal black.

There are several corrections you can make in the Primary Out room to correct the blacks. You can use the Shadow contrast slider, the Luma curve, and the settings available in both the Basic and Advanced tabs.

How you approach legalizing a clip is a combination of personal preference and the demands of the clip. Different corrections will have varying levels of impact on the mid-tones. It's up to you to decide on the best course of action to achieve the look that both satisfies the need for a legal signal and keeps the client happy.

Finally, keep in mind that video may have black levels that are not part of the picture and may mask the true black level of the image. Depending on the recording device and how the video was captured, you may have black along the edges of the frame that is darker than the black of the recorded image. The image below shows a frame of video as viewed in QuickTime Player that contains an example of "nonpicture" black.

**TIP** ▶ You can use the Pan & Scan tab of the Geometry room to temporarily crop the image to remove black borders. Remember to remove the cropping when you are finished with your corrections.

You'll adjust the black levels using several different methods, storing each correction in a different grade. Shot 1 already has four grades applied to it, all identical. You'll modify each grade using a different technique. This method will allow you to quickly switch between the different grades to see how each technique affected the shot.

1 Stop playback if necessary and position the playhead in the middle of shot 1.

2 Click the Primary Out tab or press Command-5 to open the Primary Out room.

3 Click grade 1 or press Control-1.

**4**   Use the Shadow contrast slider to bring the blacks up to zero, watching the Waveform Monitor as a guide.

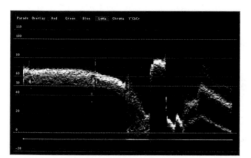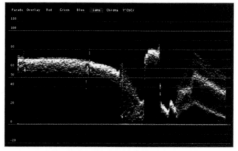

The image on the left shows the black levels before correction; the image on the right shows the levels after correction using the Shadow contrast slider.

**5**   Click grade 2 or press Control-2.

**6**   Drag the black point handle of the Luma curve upward until the black levels appear to be legal in the Waveform Monitor.

**7**   Click grade 3 or press Control-3.

**8**   Scrub the Master Lift value in the Basic tab until the black levels appear to be legal in the Waveform Monitor. Note that Master Lift affects the entire luma range, so you may negatively affect other areas of the image.

**9**   Click grade 4 or press Control-4.

**10**  Click the Advanced tab and scrub the Green Lift value until the black levels appear to be legal in the Waveform Monitor.

You can cycle through the four methods by clicking the grades or using the keyboard shortcuts. As you do so, watch both the Waveform Monitor and the preview image to see how each method affects the shot.

You should notice that adjusting the Shadow contrast slider and the Luma curve produced nearly nearly identical results. The Luma curve correction may appear to have a slightly lower contrast due to the flattening of the Luma curve, but both should look good.

Grade 3, done using the Master Lift, will generally appear brighter than the first two techniques. The first two techniques primarily affect the shadows, but Master Lift essentially raises the luma for all areas of the image—shadows, midtones, and highlights.

Clearly the Green Lift technique used on grade 4 is not suitable for this clip. Although there are a variety of uses for lifting an individual channel, it's generally used to correct an indiscriminate color cast or to create a stylized effect.

## Limiting the Range of Black Level Adjustments

Finally, if you've already corrected the overall look of the project, you don't want the broadcast-safe corrections to alter the overall look of a shot. For this shot, you'll use the Luma curve to raise the black level but limit the effect on the midtones and highlights.

1   Select grade 1 and click the Shadow Adjustments reset button.

Look at the Waveform Monitor and note where the dark wood trim falls. It creates two downward peaks that just touch the black levels.

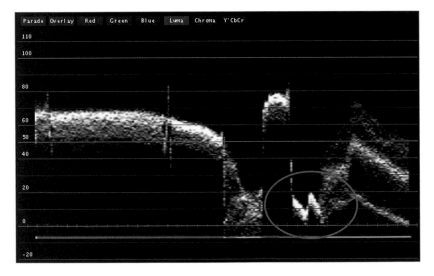

2   Select grade 2.

**3**  Drag down on the Shadow contrast slider until the area of the Waveform Monitor that corresponds to the dark wood trim matches the waveform display of the uncorrected clip.

> **TIP** ▶  You can use the Still Store feature to compare the original clip to your corrected clip. Refer to Lesson 5 for more information on using Still Store.

Switch between grade 1 and grade 2. The shadow exposure of the two should be nearly identical, yet grade 2 has corrected black levels. The black levels of grade 2 can't drop below zero. That's because the Luma curve is applied after the shadow, midtone, and highlight corrections. Since the Luma curve black point has been raised, shadow corrections can't drop below that new black point value. The Luma curve limits the range of adjustments that can be made with the contrast sliders.

**4**  Switch between grade 1 and grade 2 while watching the Vectorscope. You may notice that the saturation of the shot has increased in grade 2.

**5**  Select grade 2. Scrub the value of the Saturation field in the Basic tab while watching the Vectorscope. Adjust the value until the Vectorscope approximates the saturation of grade 1. A value of .94 worked well in this example.

## Manually Adjusting White and Black Levels

The exterior door shot had white levels that did not need adjusting. The fourth shot in the Timeline, **CU_Henry_04**, has white levels that exceed legal values by a good margin. You'll correct both the black and white levels of shot 4. Study the waveform of shot 4 for a few moments, taking note of where highlight and shadow detail fall on the scale of the monitor. You'll notice the midtone area of the Waveform Monitor is compressed so that you can more accurately measure shadow and highlight detail.

**1**  Double-click shot 4, **CU_Henry_04**, to select it.

**2**  Select grade 2.

Grade 1 will be left untouched to be used as a comparison.

**3**    Drag the black point control of the Luma curve upward until the black levels appear
to be legal in the Waveform Monitor.

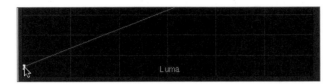

**4**    Drag the white point control of the Luma curve downward until the white levels
appear to be legal in the Waveform Monitor.

At this point, the contrast of the image will appear reduced. As the slope of the Luma
curve gets flatter, visual contrast in the image is reduced. In the next step, you'll restore
contrast by adding controls to the Luma curve.

**TIP**    To truly evaluate the effects of your corrections, you need to view your program on an external NTSC or HD monitor.

**5**    Click the Luma curve near the intersection of the fifth vertical and fifth horizontal
grid lines to add a control point.

**6**    Drag the control upward, watching the Waveform Monitor until the highlight traces
are restored to their original values.

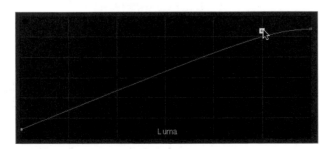

**7**   Click the Luma curve near the intersection of the second vertical and second horizon-tal grid lines to add a control point.

**8**   Drag the control downward, watching the Waveform Monitor until the shadow detail traces are restored to their original values.

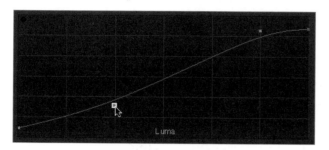

**9**   Press Control-1 and Control-2 to alternate between grades 1 and 2 to compare your work.

**TIP**  You can use the Still Store feature to compare the original clip to your corrected clip. Refer to Lesson 5 for more information on using Still Store.

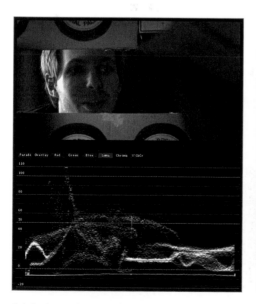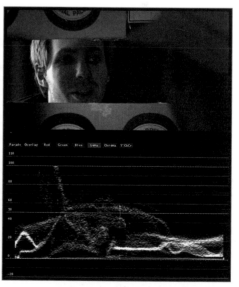

Original on left, corrected version on right.

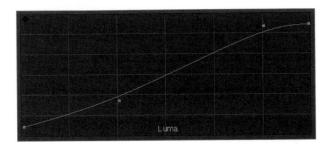

Using the steps found in the "Applying Stylized Primary Out Corrections to Grouped Clips" section earlier in this lesson, you can now apply the broadcast-safe corrections to groups of similar clips. Keep in mind, however, that it is a good idea to review each shot to make sure it falls within the limits required for delivery.

You can use whatever techniques best fit your footage and workflow. When you're finished, you can use the Broadcast Safe feature of the Setup room as a safety net to catch any stray pixels that might otherwise fall outside of legal limits.

## Manually Adjusting Chroma Levels

In addition to illegal luma levels, it's also possible to have chroma levels that exceed broadcast-safe limits. The Broadcast Safe setting in the setup room will limit chroma as well as luma. However, for this exercise, the Broadcast Safe setting is turned off, so you need to manually limit chroma levels. There are several ways to analyze chroma. The Vectorscope, Parade Scope, and Chroma Scope are all useful in evaluating chroma. For this exercise, you'll primarily use the Chroma Scope.

1   Double-click shot 2 (**MLS_Henry_02_uncorr**) to select it.

2   Verify that the playhead is on the first frame of the clip.

3   In the Scopes window, click the Chroma button above the Waveform Monitor to display the Chroma Scope.

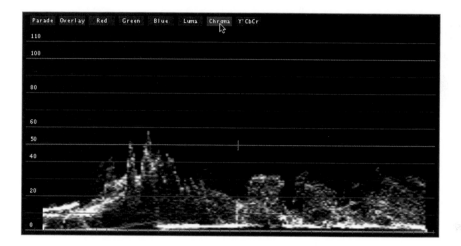

The Chroma Scope shows the combined $C_B$ and $C_R$ color-difference components of the image. A very conservative approach to chroma legalization is to reduce values above the 50% line to 50%. However, it is possible to have chroma levels above 50% in the Chroma Scope that are still legal in the Vectorscope or the RGB Parade.

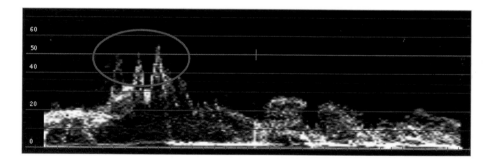

Based on the Chroma Scope, this clip has chroma values that need to be reduced. They are noted above.

**NOTE** ► The Parade Scope and the Vectorscope are also important for checking chroma legality. Generally, any areas of the Vectorscope that fall beyond the color bar targets are considered illegal. In order to fully check for legal chroma, it's best to use all three monitors in unison.

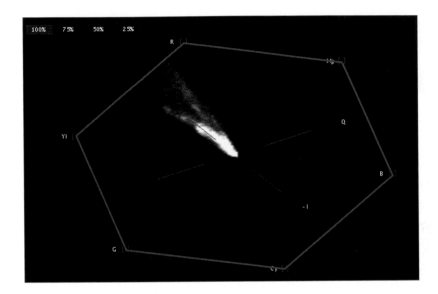

The red lines above indicate a conservative estimate of legal chroma limits. When the Vectorscope is set to 100% magnification, legal chroma roughly falls within the boundary created by connecting the color bar target graticules.

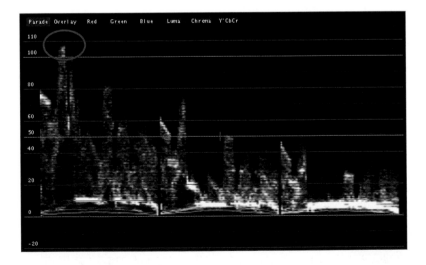

Areas below 100% on the Parade Scope represent legal chroma. The above image shows reds that may need to be corrected. (The Parade Scope shows the Red, Green, and Blue components in that order.)

**4** Use the Saturation adjustment of the Basic tab to lower the chroma of the clip, using the Chroma Scope as a guide.

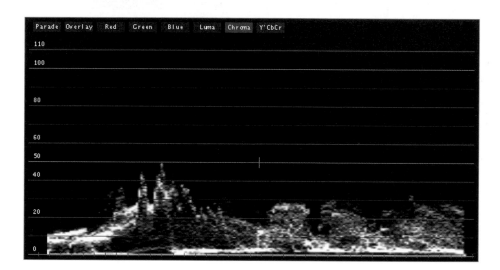

**NOTE ▶** Because Color works in RGB color space, adjusting saturation can also affect the luma values. When you're correcting for broadcast legality, it's critical to verify that adjustments in one area don't cause illegal values in another.

**5** Click the Luma button above the Waveform Monitor.

The black values have dropped below 0 due to the saturation correction. You need to raise them to 0.

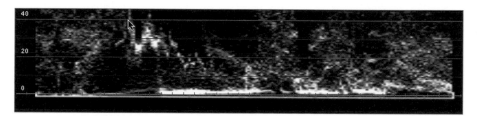

**6** Drag the black point control of the Luma curve upward until the black levels appear to be legal in the Waveform Monitor.

You've made your adjustments based on the first frame of this clip. Play the clip or step through it with the arrow keys to make sure the corrections are sufficient for the entire clip.

You can use whatever techniques best fit your footage and workflow. When you're finished, you can use the Broadcast Safe feature of the Setup room as a safety net to catch any stray pixels that might otherwise fall outside of legal limits.

**NOTE ▶** Some broadcasters require that an image be legalized in the RGB color space. In this case, use the Parade Scope to view the chroma level of each RGB channel. An external monitor using a diamond display (such as those made by Tektronix) is also an excellent way to check for out–of-gamut RGB components.

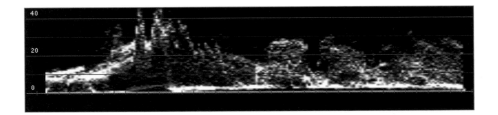

## Rendering Color Projects

In order to export a completed project out of Color, you must render the corrections to a new set of media. If you sent the project to Color from Final Cut Pro, the newly rendered files from Color will be placed into a new sequence that is sent back to Final Cut Pro. The original clips will not be modified in any way. Color provides a nondestructive, nonlinear digital workflow and is tightly integrated with Final Cut Pro using roundtrip Send To commands.

### Modifying Render Settings in the Setup Room

The basic render settings are made in the Project Settings tab of the Setup room. It's important to review these settings before beginning to render files. You need to set the location of the render folder, the Render File Type, and the QuickTime Export Codec, and decide whether renders are de-interlaced.

**1**    Open Lesson Files > Lesson 10 > **D_FinalProject_Render.colorproj**.

**2**    Choose File > Reconnect Media and navigate to Lesson Files > Lesson 10 > Media, then click Choose.

**3**    Press Command-1 to open the Setup room.

**4**    Click the Project Settings tab.

**5**    Click the Project Render Dir button.

The default directory for the project files used in these lessons will reflect the original system used to create the files.

A folder is created for each individual project within the Renders directory. You'll navigate to another folder using the Choose Project Render Directory dialog that opened when you clicked the Project Render Dir button.

**6**    Click the List View button near the upper-right corner of the dialog.

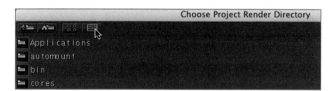

**7**    Click the Go Up button as necessary until you reach the root directory.

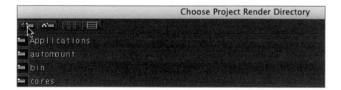

The root directory is identified by a forward slash (/) in the Directory pop-up menu at the bottom of the Choose Project Render Directory dialog.

**8** Scroll to the bottom of the list view until you see a folder named Volumes.

**9** Double-click the Volumes folder.

Any storage volumes you have connected to your computer will appear in this directory. You can create a new folder and choose it as the render directory for this project if you wish.

**10** If you don't wish to select a new render directory, click the Cancel button. Otherwise, choose a suitable location and click Choose.

NOTE ▶ The default location for the render directory is set in the Setup room, in the User Prefs tab. You can change the default render directory using the Default Render Dir. button.

**11** Set the Render File Type to QuickTime if necessary.

**12** Set the QuickTime Export Codecs to Apple ProRes 422 if ProRes 422 is not already selected.

Because this project is being sent back to Final Cut Pro, it needs to be rendered using a QuickTime codec. If the source clips use a codec supported by the Original Format option in the QuickTime Export Codecs pop-up menu in the Project Settings tab of the Setup room, you can choose Original Format as an export codec, and Color will render the video back into its original codec. If the source codec is not supported, the default codec will be Apple ProRes 422. Check the Color manual for a list of supported source codecs and more information on export codecs.

NOTE ▶ Some third-party video cards may provide additional export codec options such as AJA Kona 10-bit RGB.

**13** Set the Handles value to 00:00:00:00.

Color renders only the portion of the clip that is used in the Timeline. If you want to be able to do minor edits to the corrected sequence once it's back in Final Cut Pro, you can add handles to each clip. Keep in mind that doing so will increase rendering time and file sizes.

**NOTE** ▶ For this exercise, you do not need editing handles.

**TIP** ▶ If you send a project from Final Cut Pro to Color, several of the project settings will be preset to match the Final Cut Pro sequence. Also, some video codecs do not allow custom frame sizes.

**14** Verify that Broadcast Safe is selected.

**15** Verify that De-interlace Renders is deselected.

**NOTE** ▶ Color does a very simple deinterlace: It simply averages fields. It is unlikely that you will have Color deinterlace video when rendered.

**TIP** ▶ Deinterlacing is great for previews, especially when parked on 50i or 60i frames for long periods of time. You can have Color deinterlace only your previews by seltecting Deinterlace Previews on the Project Settings tab.

## Adding Clips to the Render Queue

When you're ready to render your final graded shots, you add them to the render queue. You can add individual clips, a group of clips, or all the clips in the Timeline.

**1** Click the Render Queue room tab or press Command-8.

**2** Double-click the first shot in the Timeline to select it. Verify that grade 4 is selected. When a clip is added to the Render Queue, the selected grade is the grade that will be rendered.

**3** Click the Add Selected button at the bottom of the Render Queue window, or press Command-Shift-A.

When a graded clip has been added to the Render Queue, a yellow bar is added to the grade in the Timeline to indicate that a grade has been added for rendering.

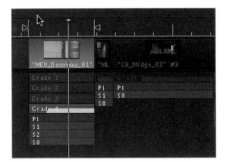

The first clip in the Timeline (shot 1) has four different grades applied to it. Each one can be added to the Render Queue.

**4**   Select grade 1 of shot 1.

**5**   Click the Add Selected button. Repeat with grades 2 and 3.

The Render Queue now lists four shots to be rendered. The shot number, name, and grade are listed to help identify which shots and grades are waiting to be rendered.

**6**   Click shot 2 (the second clip in the Timeline); then Shift-click the last clip in the Timeline to select a range of shots.

**7**   Click the Add Selected button. The additional shots are added to the Render Queue.

**NOTE** ▸ The clip under the playhead is added only if no other clip is selected. To deselect all clips, click a blank portion of the Timeline before or after the clips on the Timeline.

**8**   In the Render Queue, select Shot 1 Grade 1; then Shift-click Shot 1 Grade 3 to select a range of shots.

**9**   Click Remove Selected to clear the items from the Render Queue.

You have removed the extra grades of shot 1 from the Render Queue. The remaining shots are the final grades for all the clips in the Timeline.

**10** Select grade 4 of shot 1 in the Timeline. This will ensure that Color flags that grade as your final grade when you send the Timeline to Final Cut Pro.

> **NOTE ▶** It is critical to make sure you have the correct grade selected when adding clips to the Render Queue. As mentioned above, Color renders whatever grade was selected when the clip was added to the Render Queue. Use the Grade ID column of the Render Queue to verify that you have selected the correct grades for rendering.

> **TIP ▶** When rendering clips for broadcast, if the final video will not be limited with an external video processor, it's a good idea to return to the Setup room and select Broadcast Safe on the Project Settings tab before adding clips to the Render Queue. Doing so will ensure that any stray frames that exceed legal limits will still be made broadcast safe.

## Rendering Shots and Sending to Final Cut Pro

When you render shots in Color that are roundtripping back to Final Cut Pro, only those effects added in Color are rendered. All transitions, filters, still images, generators, speed effects, superimposition settings, and other non-Color-compatible effects from the original Final Cut Pro project are preserved within your Color project, but not rendered by Color. When you open the project in Final Cut Pro, those effects will be rendered at final output. Pan & Scan settings applied in Color are translated into their Final Cut Pro equivalent settings in the Motion tab, so you can further refine them before a final render in Final Cut Pro.

**1** Click the Start Render button.

Color starts rendering the clips. A green progress bar indicates which shot is currently rendering. The status of each shot is updated as it is completed.

The rendered media is written to the render directory you selected earlier in this exercise, or to the default render directory if left unchanged for a project.

The Timeline is updated with a green bar over each shot that has been rendered. Unrendered shots are shown with a dark orange bar.

Grades with a yellow bar have been added to the Render Queue but not yet rendered. A purple bar indicates that a grade is being rendered, and a green bar indicates that the grade has been rendered.

2   When all the clips have been rendered, save the project.

3   Choose File > Send to > Final Cut Pro.

4   When prompted by Final Cut Pro, save the project in a location of your choice.

5   Double-click the sequence named Color Sequence to open it.

NOTE ▶ If you use Send to Final Cut Pro and the current project was created using the Send to Color command in Final Cut Pro, a new sequence is automatically added to the original Final Cut Pro project. The new sequence will have its original name followed by the notation "(from Color)." However, if the Final Cut Pro project is unavailable, has been renamed, or has been moved to another location, then a new Final Cut Pro project will be created to contain the new sequence. Either way, every clip in the new sequence is automatically linked to the color-corrected media you rendered out of Color. Any original sequences are left unchanged.

6   Play through the sequence. The color-corrected clips have been placed into a Final Cut Pro project.

7   Quit Final Cut Pro and return to Color.

**TIP** ▶ In many situations, you'll want to return to Color after playing through your first graded effort to make additional corrections. It's best to open your existing Color Project and make changes to it, rather than sending the sequence Color created back to Color. Once you've finished tweaking your grades, use Send to Final Cut Pro again from inside Color.

## Using Color's Archive Feature

An archive is a compressed duplicate of the project that's stored within the project bundle itself. Whenever you manually save your project, an archive is automatically created, and it is named with the date and time at which it was saved.

The project bundle is a special kind of folder, called a *bundle*. Normally, it appears as a single file, but if you right-click a project file, you can choose Show Package Contents to reveal the bundle contents. Inside the project bundle is a folder named Archive, where archive files are stored.

1   Open Lesson Files > Lesson 10 > **E_FinalProject_Archive.colorproj**.

2   Choose File > Reconnect Media and navigate to Lesson Files > Lesson 10 > Media, then click Choose.

3   Choose File > Open Archive.

A list of Archive files is displayed.

The filenames represent the filenames of the Color project at the time the archive was created. If the Color project was renamed, the archive names may not match the current name.

If you open an archived file, the current Color project is completely overwritten with the archive file.

Before you load an older archive, it's a good idea to archive the current Color project.

4   Click Cancel to dismiss the Load Archive dialog.

5   Choose File > Save Archive As.

The default name is the current project name plus the date and time. You can edit the archive name to give it a more descriptive name.

6   Name the archive Safety Copy of E_FinalProject_Archive.

7   Click the Archive button.

8   To see the newly created archive, repeat step 2.

> **TIP**  Using archive files is a great way to be able to step back in time to a prior state of your project. Whenever you've completed an especially time-consuming grade, it's a good idea to manually save the project to create an archive that you can return to later if the project goes haywire.

## Lesson Review

1.   Are Color FX applied before or after the Primary Out room?

2.   What room has controls for setting the Render Directory and the Export Codec?

3.   True or false: The Primary Out room is visually and functionally almost identical to the Primary In room.

4.   Give three examples of Final Cut Pro items that are not rendered by Color when round-tripping.

5.   Name two ways to create an archive file.

6.   True or false: Rendered clips replace the original clips on the hard drive.

7. True or false: Broadcast-safe values may be interpreted differently by different broadcasters.

8. True or false: Color renders the entire clip, regardless of the portion used by the Timeline, when rendering grades.

## *Answers*

1. The Primary In, Secondaries, and Color FX corrections are applied before the Primary out room.

2. The Setup room.

3. True.

4. Stills, transitions, generator items, speed changes, filters, and superimposition settings are examples of items not rendered by Color.

5. Archive files are created every time you do a manual save, or use the Save Archive As command.

6. False.

7. True. Different broadcasters may impose additional limitations on the video signal.

8. False. Color renders only the portion of the clip marked by the in and out on the Timeline, plus any handles specified in the Project Settings tab of the Setup room.

# Appendix **A**
# Alternate and Advanced Workflows

In addition to the standard workflows used throughout this book, Color lends itself to a number of less common—and often more advanced—workflows used for film and video projects. This appendix gives you a brief overview of some of the alternate workflows you may encounter. It covers the following:

▶ Importing Clips to the Timeline

▶ Importing EDLs

▶ Slicing the Timeline and Using the Timeline Edit Tools

▶ Relinking Clips

## Importing Clips to the Timeline

In addition to Final Cut Pro roundtrips, you also have the option of importing media files directly to the Color Timeline. This can be useful in specific situations, such as when you are working with Cineon and DPX image sequences that Final Cut Pro doesn't support. It also can make sense if you're setting up a project for a demonstration or classroom situation and don't want to depend on Final Cut Pro round trips.

While the methods outlined in this appendix are great for 2K workflows, it should be noted that these techniques pertain specifically to 2K/Cineon and DPX workflows. Using them will interfere with the normal behavior of Final Cut Pro-to-Color roundtrips.

1   Click the Setup tab to bring up the Setup room.

2   Navigate to the media you want to import into the Timeline.

3   Click a media file to bring up additional information about the shot.

**4**   Double-click the clip you want to add to the Timeline.

The clip will be placed after any other shots that already exist in the Timeline.

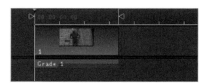

**NOTE ▶** You can also select the clip in the Setup room and click the Import button in the Timeline.

## Importing EDLs

An Edit Decision List, or EDL, is a way of representing a film or video edit. It contains an ordered list of reel and timecode data, which indicates where each video clip can be obtained in order to conform the final cut. Color imports the following frequently used EDL formats (the most common of which is CMX 3600):

▶   Generic

▶   CMX 340

▶   CMX 3600

▶   GVG 4 Plus

The steps for importing an EDL into Color are fairly straightforward, and there are several reasons for doing so. The first is to use as a cut list to cut up a master video file for purposes of color correction. In this way, you can use an EDL and the master file to simulate tape-to-tape correction. What's more, using EDLs is the only way to work with Cineon or DPX image sequences as part of a 2K workflow.

**1** Open Color, and choose File > Import > EDL.

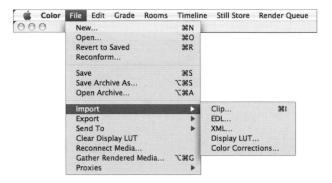

**2** Choose an EDL file from the Projects window.

The options listed below will now appear. Be sure to set them correctly for your project.

**EDL Format** Select the format of the EDL file you're importing.

**Project Frame Rate** Select the frame rate of the Color project you're about to create, which, in most cases, should match the EDL format.

**EDL Frame Rate** Choose the frame rate of the EDL you're importing.

**Source Frame Rate** Choose the frame rate of the source media.

**Use As Cut List** This checkbox lets you specify that this EDL should be used as a cut list to automatically conform a matching video master file. The master video file is then notched or cut to the EDL.

**Project Resolution** Select the resolution of the Color project you're creating. In general, this should match the resolution of the source media that you're linking to.

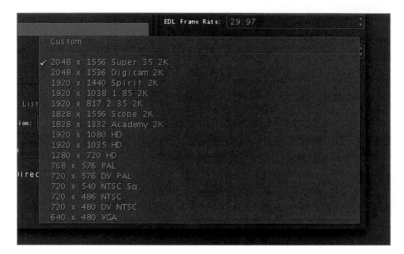

3  Specify the location of the source media you wish to link the project to. Use the Source Directory dialog to browse and select the correct directory and source media.

NOTE ▸ Keep in mind that the master video file has to be digitized first by Final Cut Pro and that timecode needs to match, and that the video should be stored on a fast hard drive.

4  After choosing all the necessary settings listed above, click Import.

A new color project is created, and the Timeline will now contain the media nicely sliced up into shots.

## Slicing in the Timeline and Using the Timeline Edit Tools

From time to time, it's useful to be able to manually override the Timeline and create your own edits. Here are some simple ways to do this.

NOTE ▶ Be very careful, because Color is not designed primarily as an editing application, and therefore should not be treated as one. Also, note that these tools are primarily made for 2K and DPX/Cineon image sequences and not for FCP-based projects; you will ruin an FCP roundtrip this way. You don't want to use these tools for video-based projects.

### Repositioning a Shot in the Timeline

1   Right-click (or Control-click) in the Timeline, and choose Unlock Track to unlock the track in the Timeline. (Normally, tracks are locked when doing a "Send to Color" from Final Cut Pro; ideally, you should be working with an unlocked Timeline.)

2   Choose Timeline > Select Tools. (Select Tools is the default state of the pointer in Color.)

**3** Drag the shot to another position in the Timeline. Keep in mind that you can't mistakenly overwrite other media, because Color is nondestructive with media.

### Deleting a Shot in the Timeline

**1** Using the Select Tools, click to select one or multiple shots in the Timeline.

**2** Press either Delete (lift delete) or Forward Delete (ripple delete), depending on the desired result. Just as in Final Cut Pro, the two different methods work in the Color Timeline.

### Using the Timeline Edit Tools

In addition to the Select Tools, Color offers a selection of standard trimming tools. Again, try to avoid editing your project in Color. These tools are provided more for last-minute or experimental cuts, rather than actual video editing.

**Roll Tool** Takes the out point of clip 1 and the in point of clip 2 and moves them in tandem. If you roll to the right you'll make clip 1 longer and clip 2 shorter.

**Slip Tool** Lets you adjust the In and Out point of a shot without affecting its duration.

**Split Tool** Lets you add an edit point to a shot by cutting it into two pieces.

**Splice Tool** Occasionally you might accidentally have created a cut, or would prefer to rejoin two shots that have been split for convenience. The splice tool joins cuts together.

## Relinking Clips

Occasionally your Color project file may become unlinked from your source media. Fortunately, it's easy to manually relink media to a Color project. When you use the Relink command, Color matches each shot in the Timeline with its corresponding media file.

### Relinking Every Shot in the Timeline

1   Choose File > Reconnect Media.

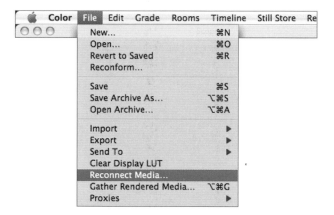

2   Navigate to the directory where the project's media is located. Click Choose.

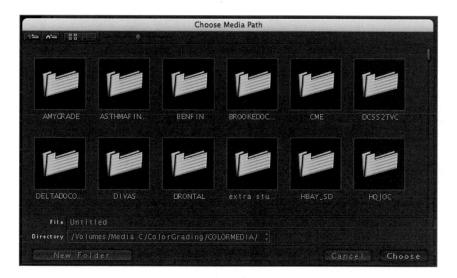

If all the required media is in one single directory, all the clips in the project will relink. However, if the media is located in subfolders or different volumes, individual clips will need to be relinked manually. See the next exercise to learn how to relink your clips.

### Relinking a Single Clip

**1** Right-click the Timeline, and choose Relink Media from the shortcut menu.

**2** Choose a clip to relink from the Select Media To Relink dialog, then click Load.

The specified media will be reconnected to your Color project file.

# B

Techniques

This appendix is excerpted from *Apple Pro Training Series: Encyclopedia of Color Correction*, by Alexis Van Hurkman. For editors and colorists who are ready to move beyond the mechanics of Color, the *Encyclopedia* is a comprehensive reference to the art, techniques, and engineering of video color correction. Available from Peachpit Press, ISBN: 0-321-43231-2.

# Setting Up a Color Correction Environment

Before you begin color correcting anything, you need to take stock of the room in which you're working. Successful color correction requires careful setup of your room, much more so than editing, compositing, or broadcast design typically requires (although those disciplines also benefit from the same attention to your environment).

This chapter suggests ways in which to set up your room and choose equipment so that you can work quickly, comfortably, and most important, accurately.

NOTE ▶ Although the advice in this chapter is most applicable to larger facilities that are willing to spend the time and money to convert existing edit suites into color correction rooms, many of the suggestions are certainly feasible even for individual operators with smaller rooms or home editors who are temporarily setting up rooms in which to color correct their video shorts.

Best practices for room setup can be accomplished in many ways; the important point is that you understand why wall color, lighting, and careful equipment selection and placement are important. Once you do, you then can decide how far to go to set up your color correction environment to meet your needs.

## Setting Up Your Room

The environment in which you're looking at your program has almost as big an effect on how the picture is perceived as the monitor you're looking at. If you're making critical color evaluations of video, it's vital to make sure that your viewing environment and monitor are up to the task.

> **NOTE** ▶ Much of the information in this section is referenced from Sony's booklet, The Basics of Monitor Technology, available online at www.sony.ca/luma. This is an excellent reference.

### Wall Color

The room in which you're working should be desaturated overall. In particular, the visible area behind the monitor should be a neutral, desaturated gray. The color may be a bit darker or lighter than 50 percent gray, according to your taste, but it should be completely desaturated (not slightly bluish or reddish, as some paints can be). Sony recommends the neutral gray area be more than eight times the monitor screen area, but it's basically a good idea to paint enough of the wall to fill your field of view while you're looking directly at the monitor.

This does two things. First, by making sure that the wall isn't any particular hue, it ensures that you'll be able to evaluate the colors of your image without outside influence. Because our eyes judge color relative to other surrounding colors, having an orange wall behind your evaluation monitor would influence your color perception, potentially causing you to overcompensate and make inaccurate corrections to the video.

Second, the contrast of images on your reference monitor is also going to be influenced by the brightness of the wall surrounding it. If the wall is either white or black, you risk misjudging the lightness or darkness of the image on your monitor as a result.

### Lighting

The lighting in your color correction room should be tightly controlled. You do not want mixed lighting in your room (light sources with two or more color temperatures in the same room), so if you have an outside window, it's best to completely darken it out using a light-blocking material. Duvetyne or other blackout fabrics work well, but whatever material you select, make sure that it blocks *all* the light, otherwise you risk allowing a bit of light into the room that's filtered to a different color, which is potentially even worse!

Once you've blocked all outside light, the interior lighting of your room should be set up very specifically. Here are some guidelines:

▶ In most North and South American and European countries, all studio lighting fixtures should have a color temperature of 6500K (D65, see Color Temperature). This matches the color temperature for noon daylight and is also the color temperature to which your broadcast monitor and computer displays should be set. One of the easiest ways to make sure your lighting is exact is to use color-balanced fluorescent lighting. You can easily obtain D65-rated tubes, and the newer electronic ballasts give instant turn-on, as well as eliminating the flicker of older fluorescent lighting fixtures.

▶ In some Asian countries including China, Japan, and Korea, the standard color temperature for broadcast monitors and studio lighting is 9300K (D93, see Color Temperature), which is a "bluer" white.

▶ All lighting in the room should be *indirect*, meaning there should be no light bulb within your field of view. It's common for lighting to be bounced off of the wall behind the monitor.

▶ Sony recommends that the indirect lighting behind (visually surrounding) the monitor be no more than 12 cd/m$^2$ (candela per meter squared, a standard unit of measurement). In other words, the ambient lighting should be about 10 percent of the illumination from a 100 IRE white signal displayed on your monitor. A more general rule of thumb is that the ambient lighting should be no more than 10 to 25 percent the brightness of your monitor displaying pure white.

NOTE ▶ This formula is intended for CRT monitors; other display technologies may benefit from different lighting ratios. Sony points out that CRT displays have higher perceived contrast with lower lighting, but LCD-based displays have higher perceived contrast with higher ambient lighting.

▶ Because the ambient lighting in the room has a significant effect on the perceived contrast of the image, some colorists recommend that your room's lighting match the ambient lighting of the intended audience's environment. In other words, if you're color correcting a program that will be watched in an average living room, then brighter ambient lighting is appropriate. If you're color correcting a program intended for an audience in a darkened theater, consider working in a darker room.

► There should be *no* light that reflects off of the front of your broadcast monitor. Any light that spills onto the face of a CRT-based broadcast monitor will lower its apparent contrast, making critical evaluation of contrast difficult. This is another reason for indirect lighting.

### Have a White Spot

Many colorists set up a *white spot* in their room. A white spot is basically a pure, desaturated area of white on the wall, illuminated with D65 temperature lighting. Think of this as a videographer's white card for your eye. Its purpose is to give you a pure white reference point with which to "rebalance" your eye. As you work, your eye fatigues, and your sense of white may drift. Glancing at the white spot lets you regain a sense of neutral white.

### Set Up Your Furniture for Comfortable Viewing

You want to set up your working surface to be as comfortable as possible, with the height of your seating, typing/mousing surface, and monitors ergonomically adjusted to avoid back pain and wrist fatigue. You're going to be sitting there a lot, so you'd better be physically relaxed in order to focus on the work. Your chair should be durable, comfortable, and adjustable (you can't spend too much on a good chair). And make sure that the client has a comfortable chair, too.

To go along with the need for a desaturated enviroment, the color of your furniture should also be desaturated. Black is a good color for the desktop, and your desk surface should be nonreflective to prevent light spill on your monitors.

### Monitor Placement

Unlike an editing suite, in which the broadcast monitor may be more for the client than for you, the reference broadcast display in a color correction room should be placed for the comfortable, ongoing viewing of both you and your client, because you're both going to be staring at it throughout every session.

For your own sanity, it's best to have a single color display to which both you and the client refer during the session. Although there are situations in which multiple displays are advantageous (for example, an extremely high-quality video projector and a smaller reference monitor for yourself), there should be only *one* display that the client refers to when describing desired changes. Otherwise, you risk having the client point at another monitor with completely different display characteristics and asking, "Can you make it look like that one instead?"

> **NOTE** ▶ Trust me, it'll happen. It's not infrequent for a client to point at the Canvas on the computer monitor and say, "Can't you make the image look more like that?" Although this is a perfectly reasonable request, it can be difficult to explain why clients shouldn't be looking at your computer's monitor.

If you've got a small room and a small monitor, placing it to one side of your computer displays is a perfectly reasonable setup.

If the size of your room (and your budget) permits, get a larger reference monitor and place it above and behind your computer's displays. This helps to prevent the light from the computer displays from creating glare on the broadcast monitor.

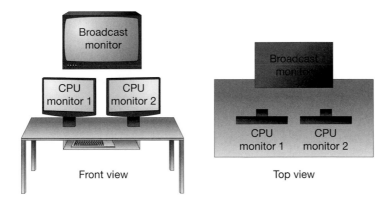

Ideal placement of the reference monitor; above, for easy viewing by both you and the client, and behind the computer monitors to prevent light spill from causing unwanted glare. The distance from the reference monitor to you should be four to six times the vertical height of the image.

In either case, you want to make sure that your reference monitor is positioned such that you're not constantly turning your head left and right and up and down every time you switch between looking at the broadcast monitor and your computer's display.

Sony recommends that the ideal distance of a viewer from the reference monitor is four to six times the vertical height of the monitor's viewable screen area.

▶ A 14-inch monitor (with a picture 8 inches in height) should be 32 to 48 inches away from you.

▶ A 20-inch monitor (with a picture 11 inches in height) should be 44 to 66 inches away from you.

▶ A 32-inch monitor (you lucky, lucky person, a picture 14 inches in height) should be 56 to 84 inches away from you.

As you're arranging your room, don't forget about your clients. They need to see the reference monitor just as much as you do. Ideally, you'll have a monitor that's big enough for them to comfortably view from a client area behind you (replete with comfy leather furniture, a working desk, Internet access, magazines, candy, and Legos to distract them from paying too much attention to you).

If your budget doesn't allow for either a huge monitor or expansive client area, then you'll need to create room for your client somewhere beside you, so you can both sit there and evaluate the image together.

## Choosing Video Hardware

When putting together a room for color correction, be very careful about the equipment you select. Because you are the last word in the quality of the video program, you need to have the cleanest, highest-quality video interface and reference monitor you can afford.

### Your Video Output Interface

You can use a variety of video output interfaces to output the program's video signal from your computer to a broadcast monitor. Rather than go into each available product in a changing marketplace, this section presents each video interface standard employed by the various video interfaces out there, as well as suggesting which might be appropriate for your application.

- ▶ S-Video is a four-pin analog prosumer video interface designed as a higher quality video interface for consumer equipment. It runs the luma and chroma of a signal separately, connected with S-Video connectors. S-Video interfaces are most commonly found on FireWire-to-DV interfaces with digital-to-analog conversion. This is not a recommended interface for professional use, but if you're working on a short program with a limited budget, it's better to use S-Video to output video to your broadcast monitor than it is to use composite.

- ▶ Y'PbPr is a three-cable professional analog video interface (as opposed to Y'CbCr, which is the standard for digital component video signals). It outputs each video component (luma and each of two color difference components) over separate pairs of wires, connected using BNC connectors (British Naval Connector). This is the highest-quality analog video signal that's typically used for professional video monitoring applications, and it's a perfectly respectable way of monitoring video for any professional application.

- ▶ SDI (Serial Digital Interface) is typically used for digital, uncompressed, standard definition video input and output. SDI is the highest-quality digital signal you can use for monitoring.

- ▶ HD-SDI (High Definition Serial Digital Interface) is the high definition version of SDI.

- ▶ Dual-Link SDI is designed as the interface for high definition uncompressed 4:4:4 video (as used on Sony's HDCAM SR equipment).

You want to make sure that, as you color correct your project, you're looking at the highest-quality image possible. If you're working on a standard definition program, either Y'PbPr or SDI would be good choices for connecting your computer's video output to a reference broadcast monitor, with SDI being the better of the two. If you're working on a high definition project, then HD-SDI is the appropriate choice. Dual-Link SDI is only necessary if your video format requires it.

To successfully monitor the picture, both the video interface connected to your computer and the video monitor must have the same interface. Most professional video monitors are expandable, so that you can purchase the appropriate interface cards for whichever format you intend to monitor.

### Choosing a Broadcast Monitor

Your broadcast monitor is your primary tool for evaluating the picture of your program. This is probably the single most important piece of equipment you will own and quite possibly the most expensive. Depending on the size of your operation, your budget is going to dictate, in large part, which monitor you'll be

Display technologies are advancing at a furious pace, so it's difficult to make recommendations that will still be valid six months later. However, when you evaluate different monitoring solutions, you should keep the following in mind:

▶ Contrast ratio—For color correction work, this is one of the most important metrics of any display technology. If your monitor won't display a wide range of contrast, including deep blacks and vibrant whites, you won't be able to make a proper evaluation of the image. The continued dominance of CRT displays for grading is owed to the extremely high contrast ratios they're capable of, which translates into very deep, rich blacks (in a proper viewing environment) and bright, pure whites. If you're evaluating a properly calibrated monitor for purchase and the blacks look gray, you should probably look elsewhere.

▶ Accurate color—Whichever display you choose should be capable of supporting the full gamut (range of colors) required for NTSC, PAL, or HD video imaging. For CRT displays, the phosphor coatings on the tube itself in part determine the color gamut of which the monitor is capable. The two current standards employed by professional NTSC displays are the SMPTE-C phosphors, and P-22 phosphors (which are slightly brighter, encompassing a *slightly* different gamut). Newer, more expensive monitors tend to use the SMPTE-C standard. One of the biggest advantages of the SMPTE-C standard phosphors is that it's easier to match the color of a group of monitors that all use SMPTE-C, which is a consideration if you're a facility with multiple suites. However, there's nothing wrong with using a high-quality monitor that conforms to the P-22 standard in a single-monitor environment. PAL monitors, and NTSC monitors in Japan, use the EBU (European Broadcasters Union) standard; however, most high-end professional monitors support gamuts for both NTSC and PAL. Color for HD monitors is supposed to conform to the Rec. ITU-R BT.709 standard, although many CRT-based HD studio monitors seem to use SMPTE-C phosphors; the monitor's electronics process the color space as appropriate.

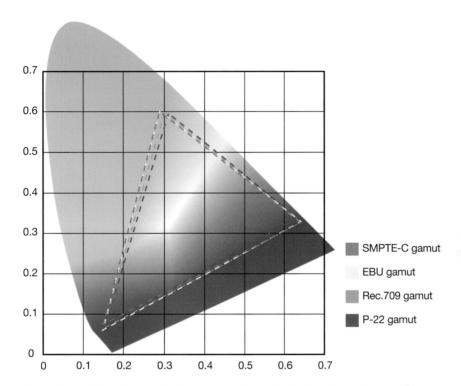

Comparison of the minute variations in gamut for each display standard currently in use, when plotted against the standard CIE chromaticity graph (a visualization of color space in two dimensions, approximated by the colored gradient in the background). The corners of each triangular gamut represent the assignment of each gamut's primaries.

- ▶ Resolution—You want a reasonably high-resolution image so that you can properly see the detail in the image you're correcting. Most high-end CRT monitors advertise 800 to 1000 lines of resolution. Other digital display technologies have fixed resolutions, based on the construction of the screen or the chip being used to create the image.

- ▶ Adjustability—You want to make sure that the monitor has the appropriate manual adjustment controls and menu settings so you can properly calibrate and set up your display for your room. At the least, a monitor should have: degaussing (for CRT displays), blue only (for calibration), under scan (for evaluation of action safe areas), bright/chroma/phase/contrast adjustments (for calibration), user selectable color temperature (with options for D65, D93 for setup), and adjustable setup/black level and component level (for setup of analog monitoring).

▶ Size—This is one of the biggest factors affecting the price of your monitor. Ideally, you'll want a monitor large enough for both you and your client to be able to sit back and watch the picture from a comfortable distance, but display technologies larger than 20 inches tend to be rather expensive (especially CRTs).

▶ Interface compatibility—Make sure that the monitor you purchase is capable of supporting (or being upgraded to) the highest-quality video signal output by your video interface.

In general, high-end CRT displays remain the favored choice for color correction work. Unfortunately, as other display technologies are taking over the consumer space, fewer and fewer manufacturers are continuing to invest in this time-honored technology. Sony, JVC, and Panasonic are three manufacturers who are still sell broadcast-quality, CRT-based products.

A few companies are developing higher end LCD display technologies in an effort to make color-critical LCD monitors. At the time of this writing, Cine-tal, Frontniche, and E-Cinema are three vendors at the vanguard of this effort.

Another option, albeit at the time of this writing a considerably more expensive one, is to outfit your room with a high-end video projector. Video projectors have the advantage of producing a huge image for viewing, and higher-end monitors are capable of very high contrast ratios when properly installed. Be forewarned that there's a significant difference in both price and quality between projectors available for the home video enthusiast and those intended for digital cinema viewing applications. Vendors you might want to investigate include JVC, Sony, Barco, Christie, and Projection Design.

As mentioned previously, some colorists are experimenting with dual-display setups, with a smaller, inexpensive CRT-based display for color-critical viewing, and a larger display of some sort for comfortable client viewing. The key to making this work is to make sure that both displays are calibrated to be as identical as feasible and that accurate calibration is maintained.

### Sanity-Checking Monitors

Another option is to have an extra set of deliberately low-quality monitors available, so that you can check to see how your programs hold up on an average television.

Some colorists also like to have a small monitor that only shows a monochrome version of the picture. This can be helpful for evaluating the contrast of the image. Because there's no color in the picture, clients are unlikely to pay much attention to it.

### Hardware Scopes vs. Final Cut's Scopes

Anyone needing to do broadcast-legal color correction in Final Cut Pro versions 5.1 and earlier pretty much needed to have a hardware scope to make a comprehensive evaluation of the video signal. These versions of Final Cut Pro didn't sample every line of video, and the software scopes presented only an approximation, useful for general adjustments, but not so good for catching every little superwhite pixel.

Starting with Final Cut Pro version 5.1.2, the video scopes are capable of sampling every single line of video, making it less necessary to have a set of hardware scopes for daily use. However, hardware scopes still have abundant uses. In particular, they're a terrific diagnostic tool for determining the state and quality of your video at various points in the signal chain. Most commonly, attaching a set of hardware scopes to the final output of your video interface allows you to sanity check the readings of Final Cut Pro's software scopes against the actual output. If there are any discrepancies, you can start working on discovering the cause, such as an incorrect setting or problem with your video interface.

Even in regular use, some hardware scopes have a wider variety of settings, options, and displays than are available with Final Cut Pro's video scopes. Furthermore, when it comes time to do a QC (quality-control check) of your program, many hardware scopes have the ability to log QC violations, along with the timecode at which they happen, in an automated fashion as you play the program through.

Bottom line, it's a very good idea to have a hardware scope available to you in your room. See Video Scopes, QC (Quality Control), Broadcast Legality.

### Video Legalizer

Video legalizers are hardware video processors that clamp or compress parts of an incoming video signal that fall outside of user-programmable limits (in other words, luma or chroma that's too high or too low) before sending the video signal out to a video deck during print-to-tape or edit-to-tape operations.

These are not intended to replace the color correction process, because it's better to adjust an out-of-range signal manually than it is to simply clip it off. Instead, these are meant to be a final wall of defense against broadcast illegality, protecting you from the occasional stray pixel, and freeing you to focus on the creative aspects of your color correction adjustments.

This is by no means a required item, but if you don't have one, you'll need to be extra careful about legalizing your programs.

See Broadcast Legality, Broadcast Safe Filter.

## Choosing Computer Hardware

If you're planning on doing color correction with Final Cut Pro, all the standard rules for choosing hardware to run Final Cut Pro apply. You'll want a good, fast computer with lots of RAM, and as much hard drive space as you can afford. Make sure in advance that the video interface you want to use is compatible with the computer model you're looking at getting.

If you're planning on mastering programs using uncompressed video, you'll need fast, accelerated hard drive storage. If your computer supports one or more ATA or SATA internal hard drives, this can be a good option. If you need more space, there are also fibre-channel based arrays such as the Xserve RAID from Apple, or one of a variety of eSATA (external SATA) array solutions.

> **NOTE ▶** For much more information on setting up a Final Cut Pro workstation, see *Optimizing Your Final Cut Pro System* by Sean Cullen, Matthew Geller, Charles Roberts, and Adam Wit (Peachpit Press).

### Input Devices

Final Cut Pro is not currently compatible with any of the third-party color correction interfaces available for other color correction applications. However, there are a handful of input devices that you can use to make your job easier:

▶   A mouse with a scroll wheel is an absolute must. You can use the scroll wheel to make fine adjustments to any slider in Final Cut Pro simply by moving the pointer over the slider you want to adjust and rolling the wheel.

▶ A set of keyboard shortcuts enables the use of a trackball with Final Cut Pro's color corrector. It's not the same as having a three-trackball interface, but because the color balance controls are essentially virtual trackballs, you might find this an interesting way to work. For the specific commands, see Color Balance Controls.

▶ A variety of USB shuttle interfaces on the market are useful for navigating the Timeline. In particular, they usually have custom buttons that you can map to the Show Next Edit, Show 2nd Next Edit, Show Previous Edit, Show 2nd Previous Edit, Show In Point, and Show Out Point keyboard shortcuts to help you flip between shots as you work.

Now that you've set yourself up with a nice little room, it's time to examine how you might approach the workflow of your project.

Excerpted from *Apple Pro Training Series: Encyclopedia of Color Correction*, by Alexis Van Hurkman. For editors and colorists who are ready to move beyond the mechanics of Color, the *Encyclopedia* is a comprehensive reference to the art, techniques, and engineering of video color correction. Available from Peachpit Press, ISBN: 0-321-43231-2.

# Glossary

**2K**  An image resolution in the RGB color space, usually 2048 x 1556 pixels for a 1.33:1 aspect ratio (Native 2K). The minimum bit depth is 10 bits (linear or log). Other 2K formats include Academy 2K (1828 x 1332, 1.37:1) and Digital Cinema 2K (2048 x 858, 2.39:1 or 1998 x 1080, 1.85:1).

**3D Color Space Scope**  A video scope displaying chroma and luma in a single view that you can manipulate in 3D space. Color is represented by one of four color models: RBG, HSL, Y′C$_B$C$_R$, or ITP.

**archive**  A compressed duplicate of the project, stored within the project bundle itself. The archive file lacks the thumbnail and Still Store image files of the full version, saving only the state of the internal project file, Timeline, shot settings, grades, corrections, keyframes, and pan and scan settings. Whenever you manually save your project, Color automatically creates an archive.

**beauty grade**  The grade you like best for each shot, indicated by a red marker in the Timeline. The beauty grade does not have to be the currently selected grade.

**bit depth**  The number of bits in a color channel; that is, the total number of values used to display the range of color by every pixel of an image. Color supports bit depths of 8-bit, 10-bit (linear and log), and 16-bit.

**black level**  (1) An analog video signal's voltage level for the color black, represented by IRE units. Absolute black, or *setup*, is represented by 7.5 IRE for NTSC in the United States. (2) Video sent digitally has no setup: The Y′C$_B$C$_R$ black level remains at the appropriate digital value corresponding to the bit depth of the video signal (represented by 0 percent on a Waveform Monitor). Modern I/O devices will insert setup for analog devices where appropriate.

**#**

**A**

**B**

**broadcast safe** Describes luma and chroma within the Federal Communications Commission's legal limits for broadcasting. Color has built-in Broadcast Safe settings that automatically prevent video levels from exceeding user-defined limits.

**B-spline** The method of editing curves that Color uses. You define the shape of the curve by dragging control points to "pull" it, like a magnet pulling a thin wire. The control points are not attached to the curve itself.

## C

**chroma (chrominance)** The color information in a video signal, ranging from the absence of color to the maximum levels of color that can be represented. Specific chroma values are described using two properties, *hue* and *saturation.*

**Chroma subsampling** Common chroma subsampling ratios in Y′C$_B$C$_R$-encoded video are 4:4:4 (the highest), 4:2:2, 4:1:1, and 4:2:0.

**Cineon** A high-quality RGB-encoded image format developed by Kodak for digitally scanning, manipulating, and printing images originated on film. Color supports 8-bit and 10-bit log Cineon image files.

**clipping** (1) The loss of luma and chroma information in an image, or (2) amother term used to describe broadcast safe. The Enable Clipping button in the Basic tab of the Primary Out room lets you set ceiling values for the red, green, and blue channels. This lets you prevent illegal broadcast values in shots to which you're applying extreme primary, secondary, or Color FX corrections.

**color balance** The relative hue and saturation values of red, blue, and green in an image's shadows, midtones, and highlights. A color-balanced image reproduces neutral colors accurately and has no color cast.

**Composer** One of the two main windows in the Color interface (the other is the Viewer). In the Composer window you'll find the Timeline as well as all the color-correction controls, which are divided into eight tabs called *rooms.*

**contrast** The distribution of dark, medium, and light tones in an image. An image's *contrast ratio* is the difference between the darkest and lightest tonal values within that image. Typically, a higher contrast ratio, where the difference between the two is greater, is preferable to a lower one.

**control surface** A color-correction device. Control surfaces typically include three trackballs that correspond to the three overlapping tonal zones of the primary and secondary color balance controls (shadows, midtones, and highlights), three rotary controls for the three contrast controls (black level, gamma, and white point), and other rotary controls and buttons.

**correction** In Color, an adjustment made within a single room. Once saved, corrections can be applied to one or more shots in your project without changing the settings of any other rooms.

**curves** A way of performing primary and secondary corrections. In the Primary Rooms, Red, Green, Blue, and Luma curves are available, and in the secondaries room are Hue, Saturation, and Luma curves. Original Values are plotted linearly on a flat diagonal line (graphed on X and Y axes). Corrections are made using B-Splines.

**DPX** Stands for *Digital Picture eXchange*. An RGB-encoded image format derived from the Cineon format, it is similarly used for high-quality uncompressed digital intermediate workflows. Color supports 8-bit and 10-bit log DPX image files.

**D**

**EDL (Edit Decision List)** A text file that sequentially lists all of the edits and transitions that make up a program. EDLs are used to move a project from one editing application to another, or to coordinate the assembly of a program in an online editing facility.

**E**

**gain** The amount by which the luma of an image's white point is raised. In Color, the master gain control found in the Basic tab of the primary rooms controls overall white level. Individual RGB gain adjustments can be made in the Advanced tab of the primary rooms and secondaries room.

**G**

**gamma** (1) A curve that describes how the middle tones of an image appear. Gamma is a nonlinear function often confused with "brightness" or "contrast." Changing the value of the gamma affects the middle tones while leaving the whites and blacks of the image essentially unaltered. Gamma adjustment is often used to compensate for differences between Macintosh and Windows video graphics cards and displays. (2) The nonlinear representation of luminance in a picture on a broadcast monitor or computer display. Applying a gamma adjustment while recording an image maximizes the perceptible recorded detail in video signals with limited bandwidth.

**grade**  A group of primary, secondary, and Color FX corrections saved across several rooms as a single unit. Applying a saved grade overwrites any corrections previously made to the shot you're applying it to. Saved grades are managed via the Grades bin, located in the Setup room.

**H**

**highlights**  The lightest values in an image; one of the three overlapping tonal zones (along with shadows and midtones). The white point of an image is the lightest pixel in the highlights.

**histogram**  A video scope that displays the relative strength of all color or luma values in an image by plotting a bar graph that shows the number of pixels at each percentage. Histograms in Color can display the RGB channels simultaneously, useful for comparing the relative distribution of each color channel across the tonal range of the image; the red, green, or blue channel in isolation; and luma only, useful for comparing two images in order to match their lightness values more closely.

**HSL (hue, saturation, lightness)**  A color model.

**hue**  An attribute of color perception. Red, blue, yellow, and green are examples of hues. Hue is measured as an angle on a color wheel.

**I**

**Internal Pixel Format**  A pop-up menu whose options determine the bit depth used for internal processing.

**K**

**keyframe**  A visual and mathematical representation of a parameter's value(s) at a given point in time. Interpolating images between two keyframes results in the animation of color corrections, vignettes, Color FX nodes, pan and scan effects, and user shapes.

**L**

**LUT (lookup table)**  A file containing information typically used to adjust the colors generated by a display. LUTs can be used to calibrate your display with hardware probes, and they also let you match your display to other imaging mediums, including digital projection systems and film printing devices.

**lift**  The amount by which an image's luma value is adjusted. In Color the master lift control, found in the Basic tab of the primary rooms, controls overall luma level. Individual RGB lift adjustments can be made in the Advanced tab of the primary rooms and secondaries room.

**luma**  Gamma-weighted luminance used for broadcast. Luma describes the exposure of a video shot, from absolute black (0 in Color) through the gray tones to the brightest white (100). Because luma and color are separate qualities, the grayscale result of a complete desaturation can be called the image's luma.

**M**

**Merge Edits**  A splicing command in the Timeline menu. It rejoins two shots separated by a through edit at the current playhead position. Using this command eliminates the need to choose a tool.

**midtones**  (1) The distribution of all tonal values in between the black and white points of an image. (2) One of the three overlapping tonal zones of an image (along with shadows and highlights). Nonlinear adjustments to the distribution of midtones are often referred to as *gamma* adjustments.

**N**

**node**  An image-processing operation used in the Color FX room. Combinations of nodes are called *node trees*. Nodes can apply different types of effects to different channels or parts of an image.

**noodle**  The link between the output of one node and the input of another.

**P**

**playback mode**  The method by which you set the Timeline In and Out points of a video for playback. The default method is the shot mode: Whenever the playhead moves to a new shot, the Timeline In and Out points automatically change to match the shot's Project In and Project Out points, and playback is constrained to that shot. In movie mode, the Timeline In and Out points are the first and last frames of the project, respectively.

**primary color correction**  A correction that affects the entire image at once. Generally, such corrections comprise three-way adjustments of the color balance, contrast, and saturation of an image for the three ranges of tonality (shadows, midtones, and highlights.)

**printer points**  Controls in Color meant to digitally recreate the optical process of light shining through a camera film negative for purposes of color correction. Color uses 50 discrete increments for red, green, and blue. Each point is a fraction of an f-stop.

**proxy**  Lower-resolution substitute used in place of the source media file in your project. Using proxies increases playback, grading, and rendering performance. Proxies are only available when working with Cineon and DPX image sequences.

**R**

**Reconform**  A command that enables an XML- or EDL-based Color project to match the editorial changes made to an original Final Cut Pro sequence.

**Render Queue**  A tab containing a list of shots in the program that you want to render. Once you've finished color-correcting your program, the controls in the Render Queue let you render the appropriate set of media files for the final output of your program, either to Final Cut Pro or to other compatible systems.

**RGB (red, green, blue)**  A color model comprising the three primary additive colors used in computer displays, scanners, video monitors, and other devices.

**ripple**  An edit that adjusts a shot's In or Out point, making the shot longer or shorter, without leaving a gap in the Timeline. The edit ripples through the rest of the program, moving shots to the right of the one you adjusted either earlier or later in the Timeline.

**roll**  An edit that adjusts the Out point and In point (the cut point) of two adjacent shots simultaneously. No shots move in the Timeline as a result; only the edit point between the two shots moves.

**round trip**  In Color, the importing of a project from Final Cut Pro for color correction and the exporting of the color-corrected project back to Final Cut Pro.

**saturation**  The intensity of a color. A completely desaturated image has no color and becomes a grayscale image. Like hue, saturation is also measured on a color wheel: It describes the distance from the center of the wheel to the edge.

**S**

**secondary color correction**  Adjusting specific elements of an image separately. Changing the color of an object in an image is an example of secondary color correction. Each shot can have up to 16 secondary operations (including Inside and Outside controls), which are made in the Secondaries room.

**shadows**  The darkest values in an image; one of the three overlapping tonal zones (along with highlights and midtones). The black point of an image is the darkest pixel in the shadows.

**slip**  An edit that adjusts a shot's In and Out points simultaneously, thereby changing the portion of the shot that appears in the Timeline. A slip edit does not change a shot's position or duration in the Timeline.

**splice**  To rejoin two shots that have been split by a through edit.

**split**  To add an edit point to a shot by cutting the shot into two pieces.

**Still Store**  A tab in which you can save freeze frames of shots and use a split-screen display to compare them with other shots in the Timeline.

**superwhite**  (1) In Color, luma levels from 101 to 109 percent, where 100 represents absolute white. (2) White that is brighter than 100 IRE. Although many cameras record video at these levels, superwhite video levels are not considered broadcast safe.

**tracker**  An onscreen control that follows an element or adjustment from frame to frame. Trackers can be used to animate primary and secondary corrections, user shapes, and pan and scan settings. There are two types of trackers in Color (auto and manual), both of which are created in the Tracking tab of the Geometry room.

**T**

**Vectorscope**  A video scope that shows the overall distribution of color in an image. The video image is represented by a graph consisting of a series of connected points that fall about the center of a circular scale. The angle around the scale indicates a point's hue, and the distance from the center represents the saturation.

**V**

**Viewer**   One of the two main windows in the Color interface (the other is the Composer). In the Viewer window you'll see your video images as well as the video scopes.

**vignette**   In Color, a mask used to isolate an area of an image. Vignettes can be adjusted to highlight a foreground subject or to shade background features, thereby focusing viewer attention. You can control the shape, softness, and placement of vignettes.

**W**

**Waveform Monitor**   A video scope that shows different analyses of luma and chroma using waveforms that are plotted left to right on a scale called the graticule. The Waveform Monitor in Color can display luma only, chroma only, Y'C$_B$C$_R$, red only, green only, blue only, RGB (Overlay), and RGB Parade.

**white level (1)**   An analog video signal's amplitude for the lightest white in a picture, represented by IRE units. (2) In digital video the representation for the lightest white in a picture, measured in percent. White levels brighter than 100 IRE/100 percent are not broadcast safe.

**Y**

**Y'C$_B$C$_R$**   The color model in which component digital video is typically recorded. The Y' component represents the luma, or black-and-white portion, of an image's tonal range. C$_B$ and C$_R$ represent the two color-difference components.

# Index

# The Apple Pro Training Series

The official curriculum of the Apple Pro Training and Certification Program, the Apple Pro Training books are comprehensive, self-paced courses written by acknowledged experts in the field. Focused lessons take you step by-step through the process of creating real-world digital video or audio projects, while lesson files on the companion DVD and ample illustrations help you master techniques fast. In addition, lesson goals and time estimates help you plan your time, while chapter review questions summarize what you've learned.

### Final Cut Pro 6
0-321-50265-5

Cut a scene from the USA Network television series *Monk*, create a promo for Seaworld's *Belief* documentary, master filters and effects as you edit a segment of BBC's *Living Color*. In this best-selling guide, Diana Weynand starts with basic video editing techniques and takes you all the way through Final Cut Pro's powerful advanced features. You'll learn to mark and edit clips, mix sound, add titles, create transitions, apply filters, and more.

### Final Cut Pro 6: Beyond the Basics
0-321-50912-9

Director and editor Michael Wohl shows how to master advanced trimming techniques, make polished transitions, work with nested sequences, edit multi-camera projects, create fantastic effects, color-correct your video, and composite like a pro. Also covers Soundtrack Pro, and managing clips and media.

### The Craft of Editing with Final Cut Pro
0-321-52036-X

Superbly fitted to a semester-length course, this is the ideal curriculum for a hands-on exploration of advanced editing. Director and editor Michael Wohl shares must-know techniques for cutting dialogue scenes, action scenes, fight and chase scenes, documentaries, comedy, music videos, multi-camera projects, and more. Two DVD-9s of professional footage and project files give students the chance to work with every genre as they learn.

### Motion Graphics and Effects in Final Cut Studio 2
0-321-50940-4

This practical approach focuses on just the parts of Final Cut Studio that editors and designers need to create motion graphics in their daily work.

### Motion 3
0-321-50910-2

Top commercial artists show you how to harness Motion's behavior-based animations, particles, filters, effects, tracking, and 3D capabilities.

### Soundtrack Pro 2
0-321-50266-3

Audio producer Martin Sitter is your guide to the only professional audio post application designed specifically for the Final Cut editor.

### DVD Studio Pro 4, Second Edition
0-321-50189-6

Learn to author professional DVDs with this best-selling guide. Build three complete DVDs, including the DVD for the Oscar-nominated *Born into Brothels* documentary.

### Color
0-321-50911-0

This guide to Apple's masterful new color grading software starts with the basics of color correction and moves on to the fine points of secondary grading, tracking, and advanced effects.

### Apple Pro Training Series: Logic Pro 8 and Logic Express 8
0-321-50292-2

Create, mix, and polish your musical creations using Apple's pro audio software.

### Apple Pro Training Series: Logic Pro 8 Beyond the Basics
0-321-50288-4

Comprehensive guide takes you through Logic's powerful advanced features.

### Apple Pro Training Series: Shake 4
0-321-25609-3

Apple-certified guide uses stunning real world sequences to reveal the wizardry of Shake 4.

### Encyclopedia of Visual Effects
0-321-30334-2

Ultimate recipe book for visual effects artists working in Shake, Motion and Adobe After Effects.

**Encyclopedia of
Color Correction**
0-321-43231-2

Comprehensive
training in the real-
world color correction
and management
skills editing pros use
every day in the field.

**Aperture 1.5**
0-321-49662-0

The best way to learn
Aperture's powerful
photo-editing, image-
retouching, proofing,
publishing, and
archiving features.

**Final Cut Express 4**
0-321-53467-0

The only Apple-
authorized guide to
Final Cut Express 4
has you making movie
magic in no time.

**Optimizing Your Final
Cut Pro System**
0-321-26871-7

The ultimate guide for
installing, configuring,
optimizing, and trouble-
shooting Final Cut Pro
in real-world post-
production environments.

**Final Cut Pro for Avid
Editors, Third Edition**
0-321-51539-0

This comprehensive
"translation course" is
designed for professional
video and film editors
who already know their
way around Avid nonlinear systems.

**Final Cut Pro 6 for
News and Sports
Quick-Reference Guide**
0-321-51423-8

This easy look-up guide
provides essential
techniques for broadcast
studios using Final Cut Pro
to edit news and sports.

**Shake 4
Quick Reference Guide**
0-321-38246-3

This compact reference
guide to Apple's leading
compositing software of-
fers a concise explanation
of the Shake interface,
workspace, and tools..

**Compressor 3 Quick-
Reference Guide**
0-321-51422-X

Learn essential techniques
for audio and video
compression, batch-
encoding, test-clip
workflows, exporting
podcasts, and more.

**QuickTime Pro
Quick-Reference Guide**
0-321-44248-2

An invaluable guide to
capturing, encoding,
editing, streaming, and
exporting media.

**Final Cut Server Quick-
Reference Guide**
0-321-51024-0

Final Cut Server delivers
intuitive media asset
management, review
and approval tools, and
workflow automation.

**Xsan Quick-Reference
Guide, Second Edition**
0-321-43232-0

Apple's exciting new
enterprise-class file
system offers high-speed
access to centralized
shared data.

# The Apple Training Series

**Apple Training Series: Mac OS X Support
Essentials, Second Edition**
0-321-48981-0

**Apple Training Series: Mac OS X Server
Essentials, Second Edition**
0-321-49660-4

**Apple Training Series: Desktop and
Portable Systems, Third Edition**
0-321-33546-5

**Apple Training Series: Mac OS X System
Administration Guide, Volume 1**
0-321-36984-X

**Apple Training Series: Mac OS X System
Administration Guide, Volume 2**
0-321-42315-1

**Apple Training Series: iLife '08**
0-321-50190-X

**Apple Training Series: iWork '08**
0-321-50185-3

# ONE SIX RIGHT
## THE ROMANCE OF FLYING

Learn more about this independent film's journey from conception to distribution at:
www.apple.com/pro/profiles/terwilliger

W W W . O N E S I X R I G H T . C O M